Towards Tolerance

Towards Tolerance

Exploring changes and explaining differences in attitudes towards homosexuality in Europe

Lisette Kuyper
Jurjen Iedema
Saskia Keuzenkamp

The Netherlands Institute for Social Research | scp
The Hague, May 2013

The Netherlands Institute for Social Research | scp was established by Royal Decree of March 30, 1973 with the following terms of reference:
a   to carry out research designed to produce a coherent picture of the state of social and cultural welfare in the Netherlands and likely developments in this area;
b   to contribute to the appropriate selection of policy objectives and to provide an assessment of the advantages and disadvantages of the various means of achieving those ends;
c   to seek information on the way in which interdepartmental policy on social and cultural welfare is implemented with a view to assessing its implementation.

The work of the Netherlands Institute for Social Research focuses especially on problems coming under the responsibility of more than one Ministry. As Coordinating Minister for social and cultural welfare, the Minister for Health, Welfare and Sport is responsible for the policies pursued by the Netherlands Institute for Social Research. With regard to the main lines of such policies the Minister consults the Ministers of General Affairs; Security and Justice; the Interior and Kingdom Relations; Education, Culture and Science; Finance; Infrastructure and the Environment; Economic Affairs, Agriculture and Innovation; and Social Affairs and Employment.

© The Netherlands Institute for Social Research | scp, The Hague 2013
scp-publication 2013-5
Text editing: Julian Ross, Carlisle, uk
dtp: Textcetera, The Hague
Figures: Mantext, Moerkapelle
            Geografiek, Utrecht
Cover design: Bureau Stijlzorg, Utrecht

isbn 978 90 377 0650 5
nur 740

Distribution outside the Netherlands and Belgium: Transaction Publishers, New Brunswick (usa)

The Netherlands Institute for Social Research | scp
Rijnstraat 50
2515 xp Den Haag
The Netherlands
Tel. +31 70 340 70 00
Fax +31 70 340 70 44
Website: www.scp.nl
E-mail: info@scp.nl

The authors of scp publications can be contacted by e-mail via the scp website.

Inhoud

Foreword

Homosexuality was much in the news at the start of 2013. In January mass protests were mounted in France against proposals to allow same-sex couples to marry and adopt children. The public expressions of discontent fell on deaf ears: in early February a large majority of the French parliament voted in favour of allowing same-sex marriage. In the same month, a large majority in the British House of Commons also voted to allow same-sex marriage in England and Wales. While the passage of these bills in France and Britain brought the equal treatment of homosexual and heterosexual individuals a step closer, the Polish parliament voted against a form of civil partnership for same-sex couples and the Russian parliament drastically curtailed the rights of lesbian, gay and bisexual citizens. If the 'anti-gay propaganda bill' is passed into Russian law, it will make providing information on homosexuality and bisexuality a punishable offence, along with organising demonstrations in favour of equal rights and possibly references to homosexuality in books and films. Many European countries and international organisations have made known their disapproval of the new Russian proposals.

Public opinion on homosexuality plays a major role in the public debate on 'gay marriage' and how it is reported in the media. How do public attitudes to homosexuality vary across different European countries? Is acceptance increasing or decreasing? And how is it possible that there are such wide differences within Europe? The Netherlands Institute for Social Research/scp addresses these questions in this report. The report explores and explains developments and differences in attitudes to homosexuality in European countries on the basis of large-scale European data sets. In which countries is acceptance increasing – or decreasing? Which countries can currently be regarded as tolerant and in which countries are there clear limits to the acceptance of homosexuality? Which factors underlie the differences? Are they caused by differences in income, education, degree of urbanisation, religion, political situation or attitudes with regard to gender? Are the differences between countries still substantial after controlling for these factors?

This report was compiled at the request of the Emancipation Department at the Dutch Ministry of Education, Culture and Science. In addition to members of the internal advisory committee, Professor Jan Willem Duyvendak (University of Amsterdam) made comments and put forward suggestions for the research plan and draft report. On behalf of the researchers, I would like to thank him for his valuable contribution and collaborative approach.

Prof. dr. Paul Schnabel
Director, Netherlands Institute for Social Research

1   47 countries, 47 opinions

The position of lesbian, gay, and bisexual citizens (LGBs) differs widely across Europe.[1] Currently, marriage between same-sex partners is allowed in several countries, while in others there is no possibility of having a same-sex partnership registered. There are as many people taking to the streets to show their support for equal rights as there are people flocking to the streets to restrict those rights. There are several European countries in which LGB individuals are respectable members of parliament, while in other European countries respectable members of parliament condemn LGB individuals.

In some parts of Europe, LGB events are proudly hosted by state officials such as ministers, mayors and members of parliament, while in others state officials obstruct or ban such events. At a time when education about homosexuality is becoming a mandatory part of the official school curriculum in some countries, other countries decry references to homosexuality in education as 'homosexual propaganda' and design laws to ban this altogether.

In addition to a wide variation in LGB policies and laws, public attitudes towards LGB people also differ widely between European countries, ranging from broad tolerance to widespread rejection. For example, the most recent Eurobarometer survey (Special Eurobarometer 393 2012) showed that in Sweden, only 2% of the population would feel totally uncomfortable with an LGB person in the highest elected political position in the country. In the Slovak Republic, by contrast, only 2% would feel totally comfortable with it. Attitudes and policies are interconnected, making attitudes an important factor in promoting equality in Europe. It is for this reason that this reports looks at this issue.

1.1   Attitudes and equality: two-way traffic

Public attitudes towards homosexuality shape the lives of millions of LGB citizens in various ways. Firstly, people's attitudes are related to their behaviour. There is a strong relationship between negative attitudes and anti-gay behaviour (Bernat et al. 2001; Franklin 2000; Patel et al. 1995; Parrott 2008). If public attitudes in a particular country are overly negative, LGB individuals face negative reactions and discrimination when looking for a job, going to school, participating in sport, accessing health care or interacting with family and friends.

In addition to the relationship between negative attitudes and anti-gay behaviour, public opinion plays an important role in the development of laws and policies. Public attitudes, policies and laws related to LGB issues are interconnected (Lax and Phillips 2009; Loftus 2001; Meeusen and Hooghe 2012; Riggle et al. 2010; Takács and Szalma 2011). One way in which public opinion shapes policies and laws is through the 'electoral connection' (Lax and Phillips 2009: 369). Politicians often have a strong desire to be (re)elected and are therefore sensitive to opinions held by large tracts of the population in order to gain popularity. Lax and Phillips (2009) show that more supportive public opinions are associated with higher probabilities of LGB policy adoption by the state, especially when an issue is prominent in the public debate. In that case, politicians are more willing to comply with the opinion of the majority (or at least a substantial part of the population) to show their democratic and representative qualities. On the other hand, the way in which policies and laws are designed and framed shapes public opinion and behaviour (Bröer 2006; Pierson 1993). Policies and laws shape the dominant public discourse, which in turn exerts an influence on everyday life. Shifts in policies on certain issues lead to shifts in the perceptions, attitudes and experiences of citizens. The interplay between policies and laws varies between countries, changes over time and depends on the political system and configuration of political parties within a country.

The relationship between attitudes and behaviour and the interconnection of attitudes and laws and policies makes public attitudes worth studying. Those attitudes are more than just individual opinions; they are one of the pillars of the enhancement of equality and non-discrimination. By studying population attitudes to homosexuality in Europe, the Netherlands Institute for Social Research|scp seeks to contribute to the policy aim of the Dutch Ministry of Education, Culture, and Science (ocw) of promoting the equal rights and safety of LGB people in Europe (TK 2010/2011). Having an insight into the stability of and changes in public attitudes and the factors that influence those attitudes provides pointers on how to address this topic when designing policies and programmes to enhance equal rights and safety.

1.2   This report

Recent cross-European reports by the European Agency for Fundamental Rights (FRA 2008, 2009, 2011), the European Commission (EC 2008, 2009, 2012), and SCP (Keuzenkamp 2011; Keuzenkamp and Bos 2007) provide reliable overviews of the current social situation and of public attitudes to homosexuality in Europe. However, due to their comprehensive and descriptive nature, these reports lack the space to explore shifts in attitudes and factors that explain differences between countries. An insight into these shifts and factors is essential when addressing this pillar of the development of policies and programmes to enhance equal rights and safety. This report therefore explores whether there are any shifts in attitudes in different European countries. Are there European countries which are moving towards more tolerance? Are there countries moving in the other direction? And are there countries where attitudes have stayed the same over the years? This report not only describes changes in attitudes within European countries, but also seeks explanations for differences between countries. Whilst seeking these explanations, specific attention will be devoted to gender issues. For example, are more tolerant attitudes to homosexuality found in countries which hold less traditional attitudes to appropriate gender roles and which have high levels of gender equality in education, economics and politics? In sum, this report addresses three research questions:

1   Which shifts in public attitudes towards homosexuality[2] can be found in European countries?
2   To what degree are gender issues related to attitudes towards homosexuality in Europe?

3 To what degree can differences in attitudes between European countries be explained by modernization, religion and policies and politics?

The questions regarding shifts in attitudes will be addressed in chapter 2, followed in chapter 3 by an analysis of the association between various gender issues and attitudes to homosexuality. Chapter 4 provides an overview of the literature on explanations for current differences between countries and tests these explanations together with gender issues in a single overarching model. Chapter 5 tries to bring the facts and figures to life by examining some actual country cases. Chapter 6 consists of summarizing, criticizing, and concluding comments. A summary in Dutch and in English is added after the last chapter.

The report draws on various existing cross-European surveys. To address the question of changes over time, data are used from the European Values Study (EVS) and the European Social Survey (ESS). Both studies are large-scale, cross-national surveys of values conducted at various time intervals in more than 20 European countries including more than 50,000 participants in their recent editions. While other large-scale cross-European studies exist (e.g. Eurobarometer, International Social Survey Programme), the EVS and ESS are the only reliable cross-European studies which include the same questions on LGB attitudes at regular time intervals, allowing for reliable analyses over time.

The EVS contains two questions on attitudes to homosexuality: whether people believe that homosexuality is justifiable and how they would feel about having homosexual neighbours. The EVS data were collected in 1981, 1990, 1999, and 2008. In order to be able to examine changes over time, only the countries for which at least three waves of data are available could be included in the second chapter of this report. A total of 27 countries completed at least three waves and were used for the analyses in chapter 2: Iceland, Norway, Sweden, Finland, Denmark, Netherlands, Belgium, Germany, France, Great Britain, Ireland, Northern Ireland, Austria, Poland, Bulgaria, Romania, Czech Republic, Slovak Republic, Slovenia, Hungary, Estonia, Latvia, Lithuania, Italy, Spain, Portugal and Malta.[3]

The ESS contains one item pertaining to homosexuality: gay men and lesbians should be free to live their own lives as they wish. The ESS collected data in 2002, 2004, 2006, 2008, and 2010. In order to be able to examine changes over time, only the countries for which at least three waves of data are available could be included in the second chapter of this report. A total of 24 countries completed at least three waves: Norway, Sweden, Finland, Denmark, Netherlands, Belgium, Germany, France, Great Britain, Ireland, Austria, Switzerland, Poland, Russian Federation, Ukraine, Bulgaria, Czech Republic, Slovak Republic, Slovenia, Hungary, Estonia, Greece, Spain and Portugal.

Since the EVS contains more questions on gender attitudes, the in-depth analyses of the factors explaining different levels of acceptance of homosexuality are conducted using the EVS data only. The data from the 2008 round of data collection were used for the analyses. Since the prerequisite of having completed at least three waves of data collection was not necessary for the analyses of the relationship between gender issues and homosexuality, an additional eighteen countries could be included in the analyses: Albania, Armenia, Bosnia-Herzegovina, Belarus, Croatia, Cyprus, Northern Cyprus,

Georgia, Greece, Luxembourg, Moldova, Montenegro, Russian Federation, Serbia, Switzerland, Turkey, Ukraine and Macedonia.[4]
More information regarding the data collection and research methodology of both studies can be found online at www.scp.nl, www.europeansocialsurvey.org and www.europeanvaluesstudy.eu.

2 Exploring shifts and differences

Public attitudes are not set in stone, but are subject to change. Previous studies conducted in Europe and the United States (us) have shown substantial changes in attitudes towards homosexuality over time (e.g. Hadler 2012; Loftus 2001; Van den Meerendonk and Scheepers 2006). This chapter elaborates on these academic papers by providing an overview of the changes that have taken place in different European countries since the beginning of the 1980s. Which countries are becoming increasingly tolerant? Are there European countries which are moving towards greater intolerance? And are there countries where no change is taking place, or where previous changes in attitudes have come to an end?

Below, all percentages and developments are presented, but only highlights are discussed. After each section, a graph of Europe summarizing the overall findings is presented. When examining multiple attitudes across multiple years for 27 countries, it is not possible to discuss all similarities and differences between countries and years separately. For this discussion, countries are clustered for sheer heuristic purposes ('in the weakest sense', according to Castles and Obinger 2008). This means that without wanting to imply that a geographical/historical dimension is a meaningful dimension when examining attitudes to homosexuality, the figures are presented along geographical and historical lines across Europe: North, West, Central/East, and South.[5]

Figure 2.1

2.1   Shifts since the 1980s

Acceptance of homosexuality

Ever since the first edition of the EVS was published in 1981, participants have given their responses to the question 'Do you think that homosexuality can always be justified, never be justified, or something in between?'. The result is often interpreted as a measure of general acceptance of homosexuality.

Figure 2.2

Mean scores on justification of homosexuality, per region per EVS round; higher scores indicate more justification[a, b]

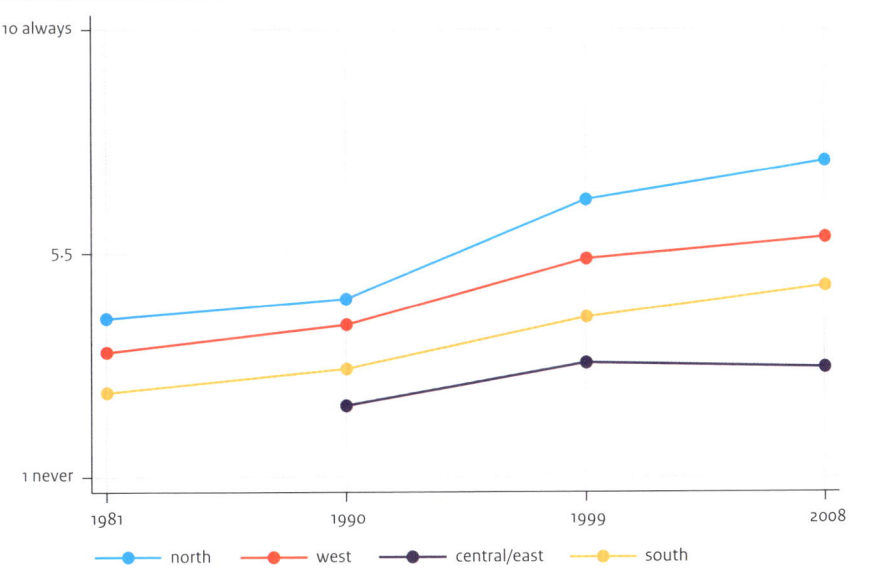

a   Appendix B, table 1A shows which changes in attitudes between years are significant.
b   The question in the EVS is: 'Please tell me for each of the following statements whether you think it can always be justified, never be justified, or something in between…[homosexuality]'. Answers were given on a 10-point scale (1 = never, 10 = always).

Source: EVS '81, '90, '99, '08

In all European regions, public attitudes towards homosexuality have changed over the last 30 years. European citizens consider homosexuality more justifiable in 2008 than in 1981/1990. Where in 1981/1990 all regions had average attitudes that were clearly below the midpoint of the scale (indicating intolerant attitudes to homosexuality), this is currently only the case in Central/East and in Southern Europe. The biggest change in attitudes took place between 1990 and 1999 in the various regions.

Figures combining countries in a region readily obscure differences between countries within regions. Therefore, the analyses are repeated on country level.

Figure 2.3

Mean scores on justification of homosexuality, per country per EVS round (1981, 1990, 1999, and 2008); higher scores indicate more justification[a, b]

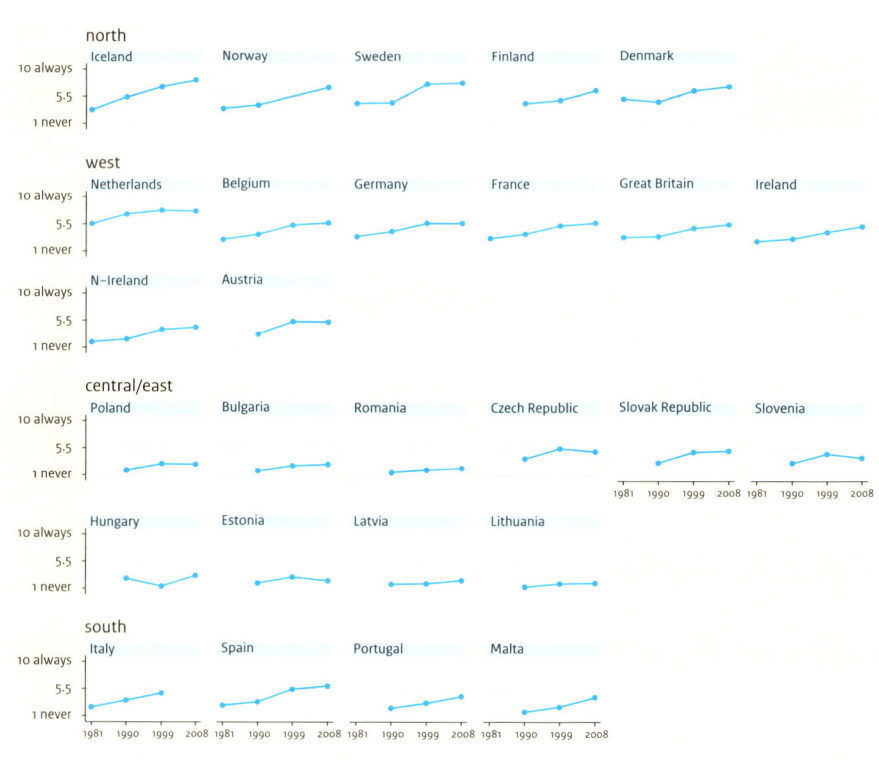

a   Appendix B, table 1A shows which changes in attitudes between years are significant.
b   The question in the EVS is: 'Please tell me for each of the following statements whether you think it can always be justified, never be justified, or something in between...[homosexuality]'. Answers were given on a 10-point scale (1 = never, 10 = always).

Source: EVS'81, EVS'90, EVS'99, EVS'08[6]

Table 2.1

Percentage of inhabitants thinking that homosexuality is never justified (answer 1)[a, 7]

	1981	1990	1999	2008	difference last and first year (percentage points)
Northern Europe					
Iceland	48	24	12	6	42
Norway	50	45	-	12	38
Sweden	39	37	9	12	27
Finland	-	32	29	16	16
Denmark	38	36	21	12	26
Western Europe					
The Netherlands	25	13	7	8	17
Belgium	52	41	27	16	36
Germany	45	36	19	17	28
France	52	40	23	19	33
Great Britain	47	40	25	23	24
Ireland	61	51	38	26	35
Northern Ireland	66	65	42	31	35
Austria	-	48	26	25	23
Central/East Europe					
Poland	-	77	60	53	24
Bulgaria	-	80	60	55	25
Romania	-	86	80	67	19
Czech Republic	-	46	27	28	18
Slovak Republic	-	52	24	20	32
Slovenia	-	60	42	47	13
Hungary	-	73	88	53	20
Estonia	-	76	57	64	12
Latvia	-	82	77	63	19
Lithuania	-	88	78	70	18
Southern Europe					
Italy	66	46	30	-	36
Spain	57	47	22	17	40
Portugal	-	65	44	30	35
Malta	-	83	61	41	42

a   The question in the EVS is: 'Please tell me for each of the following statements whether you think it can always be justified, never be justified, or something in between...[homosexuality]'. Answers were given on a 10-point scale (1 = never, 10 = always).

Source: EVS'81; EVS'90; EVS'99; EVS'08

Figure 2.3 confirms the previous findings: public attitudes towards homosexuality have changed considerably over the last 30 years in Europe. In all countries, without exception, public opinion on homosexuality is more tolerant in 2008 than in 1981/1990. To summarize this finding in a very rough way: at the start of the EVS data collection, about half the citizens in the participating countries considered homosexuality never to be justified. This proportion had shrunk to a third by 2008. On average, rejection of homosexuality decreased by about 11 percentage points every nine years. However, the pace, timing and direction of the change depends on the specific country.

In the Northern region of Europe, attitudes towards homosexuality were relatively tolerant at beginning of EVS data collection and kept on moving towards more tolerance subsequently. In 1981, levels of intolerance varied between 38% (Denmark) and 50% (Norway) of the population who believed that homosexuality should never be justified. These percentages subsequently shrank, and now vary between 6% (Iceland) and 16% (Finland). Tolerance increased in Iceland, in particular: where in 1981, 48% of the population considered homosexuality never to be justified, this had dropped to 6% by 2008. Despite the already relatively tolerant attitudes in 1999, almost all northern countries (except Sweden) continued to move towards more tolerance between 1999 and 2008. The lack of progress in Sweden is not very surprising considering the relatively high levels of tolerance found in 1999, leaving less scope for further progress.

In 1981, levels of tolerance varied considerably within Western Europe. The percentages believing that homosexuality could never be justified ranged from 45% (Germany) to 66% (Northern Ireland), with the Netherlands being an exception (25%). Nowadays, the percentages range from 16% (Belgium) to 31% (Northern Ireland), with the Netherlands again being atypical with 8%. The average level of tolerance continued to increase in the Western region during all time frames, but many national differences were found. Half the Western countries (Belgium, France, Great Britain and Ireland) continued to move towards more tolerance between 1999 and 2008, while in the other half (the Netherlands, Germany, Austria and Northern Ireland), the initial progress towards more tolerance between 1981 and 1999 came to an end. For some countries, especially the Netherlands, the lack of recent progress might be related to high levels of tolerance reached in the 1990s. But the lack of progress in Northern Ireland and Austria, where between a quarter and a third of the population believe homosexuality can never be justified, cannot be attributed to these 'ceiling effects'.

The Central/Eastern region of Europe joined the EVS for the first time in 1990. In that year, the vast majority of the population in Poland, Bulgaria, Romania, Slovenia, Hungary, Estonia, Latvia and Lithuania believed that homosexuality could never be justified (ranging from 60% in Slovenia to 88% in Lithuania). Regional exceptions were the Czech Republic and Slovak Republic, with around half the population (46% and 52%, respectively) believing that homosexuality could never be justified. In addition to the initial lack of tolerance in this region, there is also a lack of progress over the last nine years, with no change in the average level of attitudes in Central/Eastern Europe. Three countries moved towards more tolerance (Romania, Hungary and Latvia), while in four countries public opinion stayed the same (Poland, Bulgaria, Slovak Republic and Lithuania), and in three countries public opinion became more intolerant (Czech Republic, Slovenia and Estonia). Despite the lack of current progress or recent decrease in tolerance, the Slovak Republic and Czech Republic retain their position as relatively tolerant countries in Central/Eastern Europe. The current findings in the Baltic countries and Romania are more unsettling. The lack of movement towards more tolerance (Lithuania) or even a move towards more intolerance (Estonia) leaves these countries with a large majority believing that homosexuality can never be justified.

In 1981/1990, the majority of citizens in Southern Europe believed that homosexuality could never be justified. The levels of tolerance were comparable to those in Central/Eastern Europe. This was especially true in Malta, where in 1990 83% of the population thought that homosexuality could never be justified. However, in contrast to Central/Eastern Europe, much has changed in the South. Southern Europe is still not the most tolerant region in Europe, but tolerance in all four countries included has increased and continued to increase. Intolerant attitudes have fallen by 40 percentage points in Spain and 42 percentage points in Malta. This produces current levels of intolerance varying between 17% (Spain) and 41% (Malta).

The developments discussed above are summarized in graph form in Figure 2.4.

Figure 2.4

in 1981   in 1990

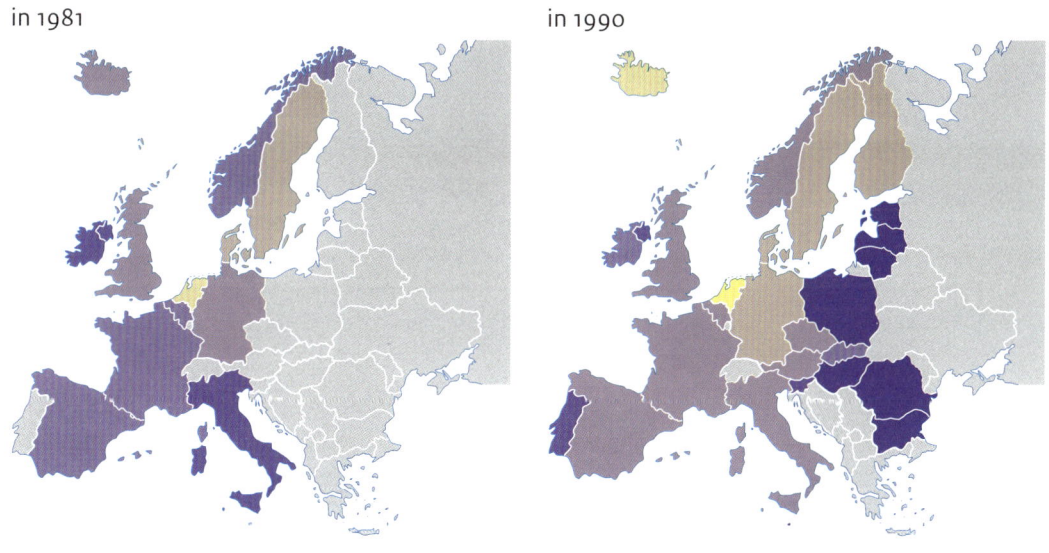

Figure 2.4 (continued)

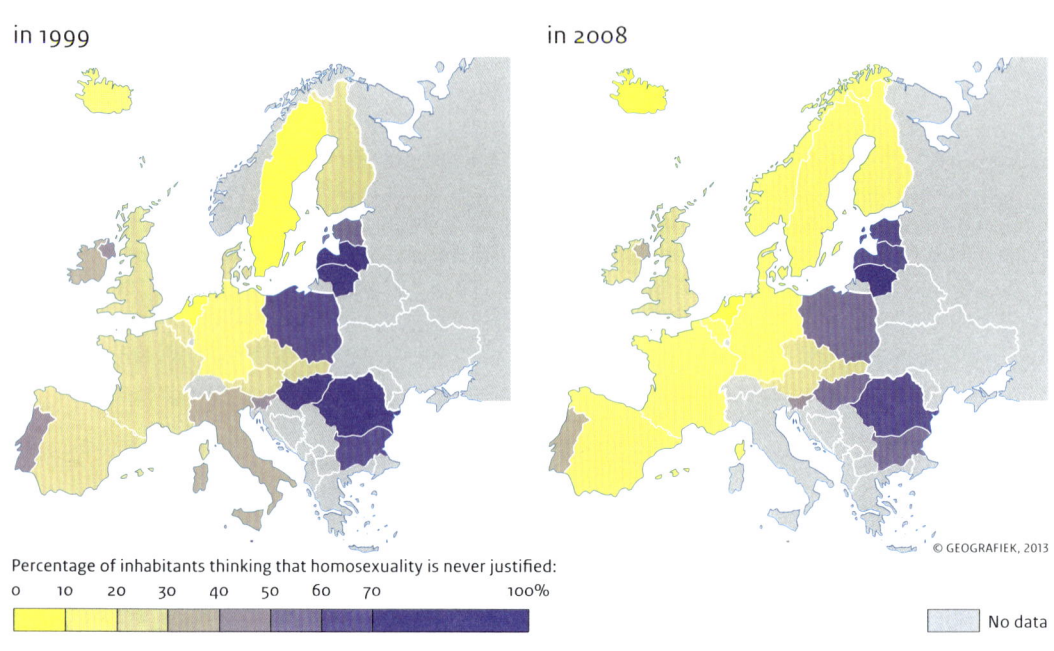

| in 1999 | in 2008 |

© GEOGRAFIEK, 2013

Percentage of inhabitants thinking that homosexuality is never justified:

0   10   20   30   40   50   60   70   100%

No data

Not in my back yard
The item measuring justification of homosexuality taps into abstract beliefs about homosexuality. In 1990, a new item reflecting attitudes to homosexual individuals was added to the questionnaire. Respondents indicated for various groups of people whether they would object to having them as neighbours. This measure reflects people's acceptance of homosexuality at close quarters.

Figure 2.5

Mean scores on whether or not participants mention homosexuals as people they do not want as neighbours, per region per EVS round; lower scores indicate more tolerant attitudes[a, b]

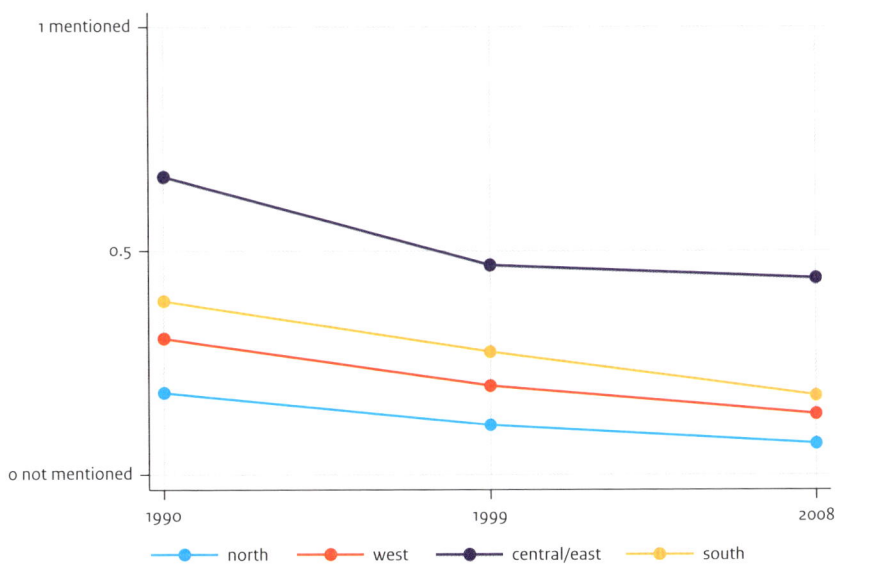

a   Appendix B, table 1B shows which changes in attitudes between years are significant.
b   The question in the EVS is: 'On this list are various groups of people. Could you please sort out any that you would not like to have as neighbours? ... [homosexuals]'. Answers were given on a 2-point scale (1 = mentioned, 0 = not mentioned).

Source: EVS'90; EVS'99; EVS'08

Just as the percentages who believe that homosexuality can never be justified have fallen over the last 30 years, so increasingly tolerant attitudes are found when the portion of the population who cite homosexual individuals as unwanted neighbours is taken in account. The number of participants indicating that they would not want a gay neighbour has fallen in all four European regions. The biggest change took place between 1990 and 1999. After that, especially in the Central/Eastern region, the trend towards more tolerance became less pronounced. Country-level analyses examine the variance between the countries within the regions.

Figure 2.6

Mean scores on whether or not participants mention homosexuals as people they do not want as neighbours, per country per EVS round; lower scores indicate more tolerant attitudes[a, b]

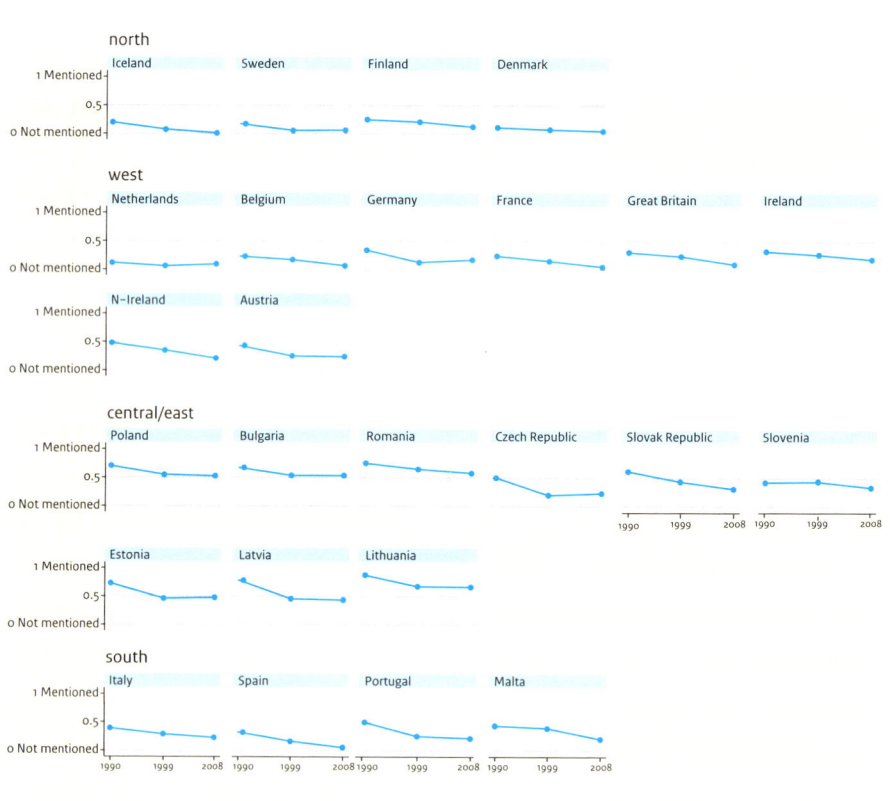

a   Appendix B, table 1B shows which changes in attitudes between years are significant.
b   The question in the EVS is: 'On this list are various groups of people. Could you please sort out any that you would not like to have as neighbours? ... [homosexuals]'. Answers were given on a 2-point scale (1 = mentioned, 0 = not mentioned).

Source: EVS'90; EVS'99; EVS'08[8]

Table 2.2

Percentage of inhabitants who mention homosexuals as people they do not want as neighbours[9, a]

	1990	1999	2008	difference first and last year (percentage points)
Northern Europe				
Iceland	20	8	2	18
Sweden	18	6	7	15
Finland	25	21	13	12
Denmark	12	8	6	6
Western Europe				
The Netherlands	12	6	10	2
Belgium	24	17	7	17
Germany	34	13	17	17
France	24	16	6	18
Great Britain	31	24	10	21
Ireland	33	27	19	14
Northern Ireland	48	35	21	27
Austria	43	25	24	19
Central/Eastern Europe				
Poland	71	55	53	18
Bulgaria	68	54	54	14
Romania	75	65	58	17
Czech Republic	51	20	23	28
Slovak Republic	62	44	32	30
Slovenia	43	44	34	9
Estonia	73	46	48	25
Latvia	78	46	44	34
Lithuania	87	68	67	20
Southern Europe				
Italy	39	29	23	16
Spain	32	16	5	27
Portugal	50	25	22	28
Malta	44	40	21	23

a   The question in the EVS is: 'On this list are various groups of people. Could you please sort out any that you would not like to have as neighbours? ... [homosexuals]'. Answers were given on a 2-point scale (1 = mentioned, 0 = not mentioned).

Source: EVS'90; EVS'99; EVS'08

At country level, the figures show a more tolerant Europe in 2008 than in 1990, with no exceptions. On average, the percentage of people not wanting a 'gay neighbour' fell by 11 percentage points every nine years. When the question was introduced in the EVS, around 40% of citizens from the countries included mentioned homosexual individuals as unwanted neighbours. This percentage had gone down to 25% by 2008. Once again, however, levels of tolerance and changes vary widely between countries.

In the early 1990s, in line with the findings regarding the justification of homosexuality, no widespread intolerance was found in the North and attitudes became more tolerant over time. In 2008, the percentages not wanting homosexual neighbours ranged from 2% in Iceland to 13% in Finland. Iceland illustrates that high levels of tolerance do not by definition hinder progress towards greater tolerance.

In the Western region of Europe, the percentages not wanting a homosexual neighbour varied widely in 1990, ranging from 12% in the Netherlands to 48% in Northern Ireland. Most of these percentages have fallen substantially over the last 20 years and the regional level of tolerance has continued to increase. In 2008, 10% or less reported homosexual individuals as unwanted neighbours in four countries (Netherlands, Belgium, France and Great Britain), and between 17% and 24% of the population reported this group as unwanted neighbours in Germany, Ireland, Northern Ireland and Austria. Focusing on more recent changes, the Netherlands and Germany show a (small) increase in intolerance. In the case of the Netherlands, this is probably due to a 'ceiling effect'. Tolerance in four other Western countries rose between 1999 and 2008: Belgium, France, Great Britain and Ireland.

In the early 1990s, the majority of the population in the participating Central/Eastern countries did not want to have a homosexual neighbour, with Slovenia as the exception (43%). In contrast to the figures for justification of homosexuality, none of the Central/Eastern countries moved towards more intolerance. In 2008, four countries still had a majority who rejected having homosexual people as neighbours, but in five countries this was no longer the case. The average level of tolerance continued to increase in this region, but there are many country-level differences. Latvia (dropping from 78% to 44% reporting homosexuals as unwanted neighbours) and Slovakia (down from 62% to 32%) changed substantially. However, in the majority of the Central/Eastern countries the change happened between 1990 and 1999 and did not persist.

In line with figures reflecting justification of homosexuality, the attitude towards having homosexuals as neighbours have become steadily more tolerant in Southern Europe. Around a third (Spain) to half (Portugal) of the population of the countries included in the survey did not want homosexual neighbours in 1990. Twenty years later, these percentages ranged from 5% (Spain) to 23% (Italy). The change in public attitudes was particularly marked in Portugal (intolerance down from 50% to 22%) and Spain (from 32% to 5%). In Italy and Portugal, no further change in attitudes occurred between 1999 and 2008, while in Spain and Malta tolerance continued to increase.

Figure 2.7 summarizes the findings discussed in the previous section.

Figure 2.7

in 1990

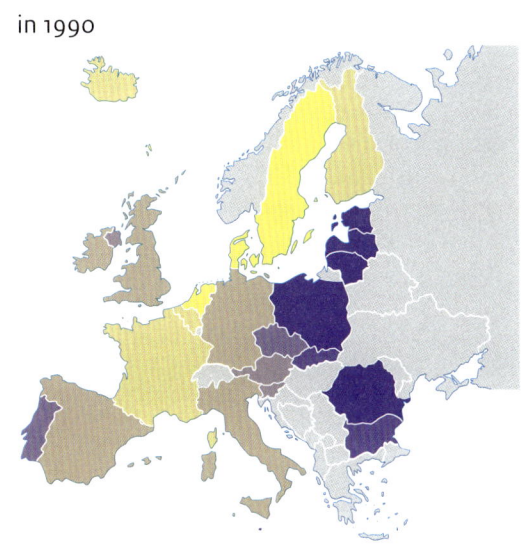

in 1999   in 2008

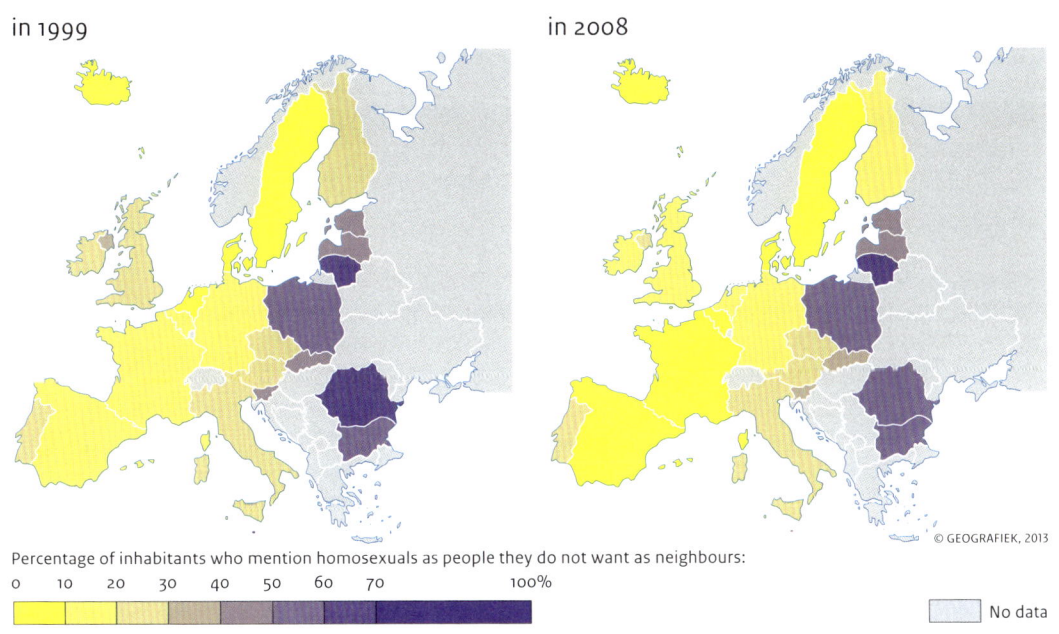

© GEOGRAFIEK, 2013

Percentage of inhabitants who mention homosexuals as people they do not want as neighbours:

0   10   20   30   40   50   60   70   100%

No data

Source: EVS '90, '99, '08

2.2   Focusing on shifts in the last decade

As shown, substantial changes have taken place in public attitudes towards homosexuality in many European countries during the last 30 years, especially between 1990
and 1999. While the long timespan of almost 30 years is a major benefit of the EVS data,
one drawback is that the EVS only collects data once every nine years. As a result, EVS
data do not allow close examination of recent changes in attitudes. The European Social
Survey (ESS) does offer that possibility. Started in 2002, the ESS collects data every two
years. Since the ESS also contains an item to measure attitudes to homosexuality ('gay
men and lesbians should be free to live their own lives as they wish'), the data do permit
close examination of changes during the first decade of the new millennium.

Figure 2.8

Mean scores on whether gay men and lesbians should be free to live their lives as they wish,
per region per ESS round; higher scores indicate more tolerant attitudes[a, b]

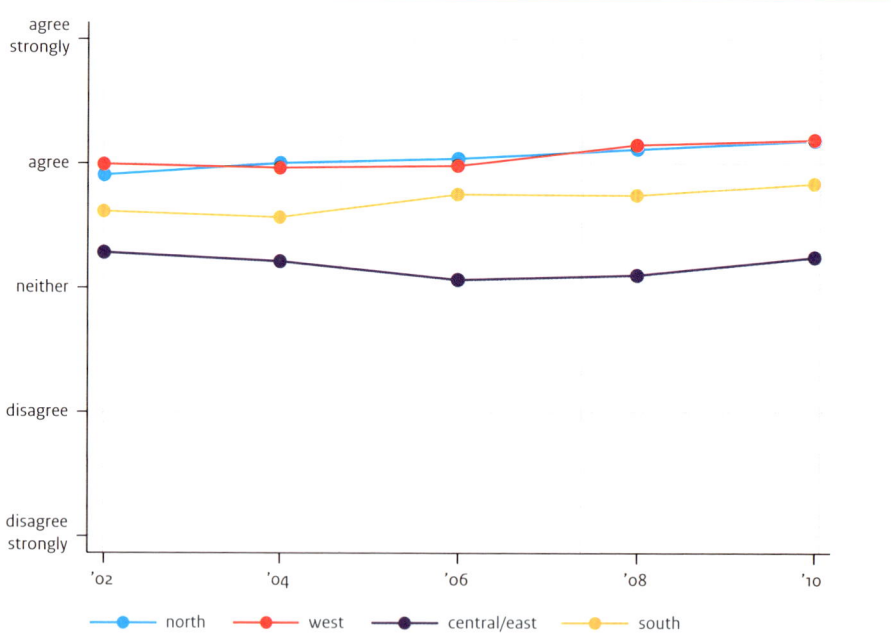

a   Appendix B, table 1c shows which changes in attitudes between years are significant.
b   The question in ESS was: 'Using this card, please say to what extent you agree or disagree with
   each of the following statements: ... Gay men and lesbians should be free to live their own lives as
   they wish'. Answers were given on a 5-point scale (1 = disagree strongly; 5 = agree strongly).

Source: ESS '02; ESS'04; ESS'06; ESS'08; ESS'10

The first decade of the new millennium can be broadly characterized as a period in which attitudes towards homosexuality did not change substantially. The regional lines fluctuate a little, but no clear trend towards substantially more tolerance or intolerance can be observed. However, the regional-level analysis might overlook differences between individual countries within regions.

Figure 2.9

Mean scores on whether gay men and lesbians should be free to live their lives as they wish; higher scores indicate more tolerant attitudes (1 = disagree strongly; 5 = agree strongly)[a, b]

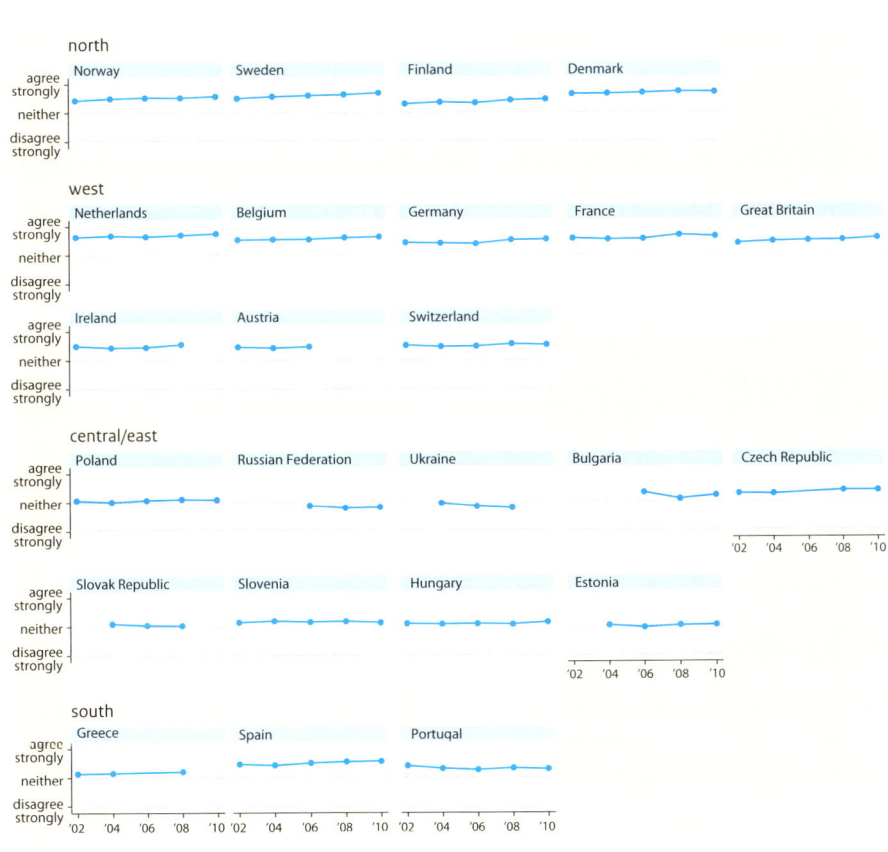

a   Appendix B, table 1c shows which changes in attitudes between years are significant.
b   The question in ess was: 'Using this card, please say to what extent you agree or disagree with each of the following statements: ... Gay men and lesbians should be free to live their own lives as they wish'. Answers were given on a 5-point scale (1 = disagree strongly; 5 = agree strongly).

Source: ESS´02; ESS'04; ESS'06; ESS'08; ESS'10

Table 2.3

Percentage of inhabitants who believe that gay men and lesbians should be free to live their lives as they wish (percentages agree or completely agree)[10, a]

| | year | | | | | difference first and last year |
	2002	2004	2006	2008	2010	(percentage points)
Northern Europe						
Norway	76	78	81	79	84	8
Sweden	82	84	86	86	90	8
Finland	62	63	64	68	75	13
Denmark	89	88	88	89	90	1
Western Europe						
Netherlands	88	89	88	91	93	5
Belgium	80	79	80	85	87	2
Germany	75	75	71	82	83	8
France	79	76	78	86	83	4
Great Britain	76	76	79	81	85	9
Ireland	83	78	81	86	-	3
Austria	74	71	72	-	-	2
Switzerland	80	76	77	82	83	3
Central/Eastern Europe						
Poland	46	43	46	51	48	2
Russian Federation	-	-	31	30	29	-3
Ukraine	-	37	31	33	-	-4
Bulgaria	-	-	62	51	55	-7
Czech Republic	60	59	-	66	67	7
Slovak Republic	-	47	41	43	-	-4
Slovenia	52	55	55	58	53	1
Hungary	48	51	47	44	49	1
Estonia	-	42	37	41	43	1
Southern Europe						
Greece	51	53	-	52	-	1
Spain	72	74	77	78	82	10
Portugal	74	62	61	66	63	-11

a   The question in ESS was: 'Using this card, please say to what extent you agree or disagree with each of the following statements: ... Gay men and lesbians should be free to live their own lives as they wish'. Answers were given on a 5-point scale (1 = disagree strongly; 5 = agree strongly).

Source: ESS '02; ESS '04; ESS '06; ESS '08; ESS '10

Country-level analyses also show relatively flat lines, indicating a lack of major changes in attitudes between 2002 and 2010. Although this general picture applies to all countries included in the study, some differences between times and places can be found (see also Appendix B, table 1C).

In Northern Europe, attitudes were relatively tolerant in 2002 and became more tolerant by 2010. No exceptions were found to this trend. Currently, three-quarters or more agrees that gay men and lesbians should be free to live their lives as they wish. Not all change took place at the same time and pace in the various countries.
Comparable shifts were found in Western Europe. In some countries, attitudes become more tolerant or intolerant in certain periods, but overall attitudes are relatively stable or become slightly more tolerant. Currently, in all Western European countries included in the study, more than 80% of the population believes that gay men and lesbian women should be free to live their own lives as they wish.[11] No country in Western Europe reported a more negative attitude towards homosexuality in 2010 than in 2002, but decreasing levels of tolerance were found in several countries during certain periods. In other Western European countries periods of increasing tolerance are found. A lack of movement towards more tolerance in some countries is probably due to the already high levels of tolerance.
A different picture emerges when shifts in attitudes in Central/Eastern Europe are considered. At regional level, attitudes towards homosexuality became more negative between 2002 and 2006, after which they became more tolerant between 2006 and 2010. In most Central/Eastern European countries, attitudes to homosexuality stay at the same level – one which can be qualified as relatively intolerant, with a minority or a small majority of its citizens agreeing that gay men and lesbians should be free to live their own lives as they wish. Exceptions to this overall picture are the Czech Republic (67% tolerant) in the tolerant direction, and Ukraine and Russia (33% and 29% tolerant, respectively) in the intolerant direction. While no country showed consistently increasing intolerance in attitudes, Ukraine showed a decrease in tolerant attitudes during a certain period without a preceding or following increase, and four countries showed no changes at all. Two countries had one period of increasingly tolerant attitudes without any decrease (Poland and Czech Republic).
The regional picture for Southern Europe shows increases in tolerance between 2004 and 2006, and again between 2008 and 2010. However, country-level analyses shows dissimilar patterns between the Southern European countries in the study. In Greece, nothing changed: in 2002, half the Greek population agreed that gay men and lesbians should be free to live their own lives as they wish, and in 2008 this was still the case. In Spain, progress towards more tolerance was found, with attitudes to homosexuality turning more tolerant between 2002 and 2006. In Portugal, shifts in attitudes went in the other direction, with tolerance levels decreasing between 2002 and 2004 and between 2008 and 2010. This resulted in a fall in the percentage of the Portuguese population agreeing that gay men and lesbians should be free to live their own lives as they wish from 74% to 63%.

Figure 2.10 presents a graphical summary of the differences between 2002 and 2010.

Figure 2.10

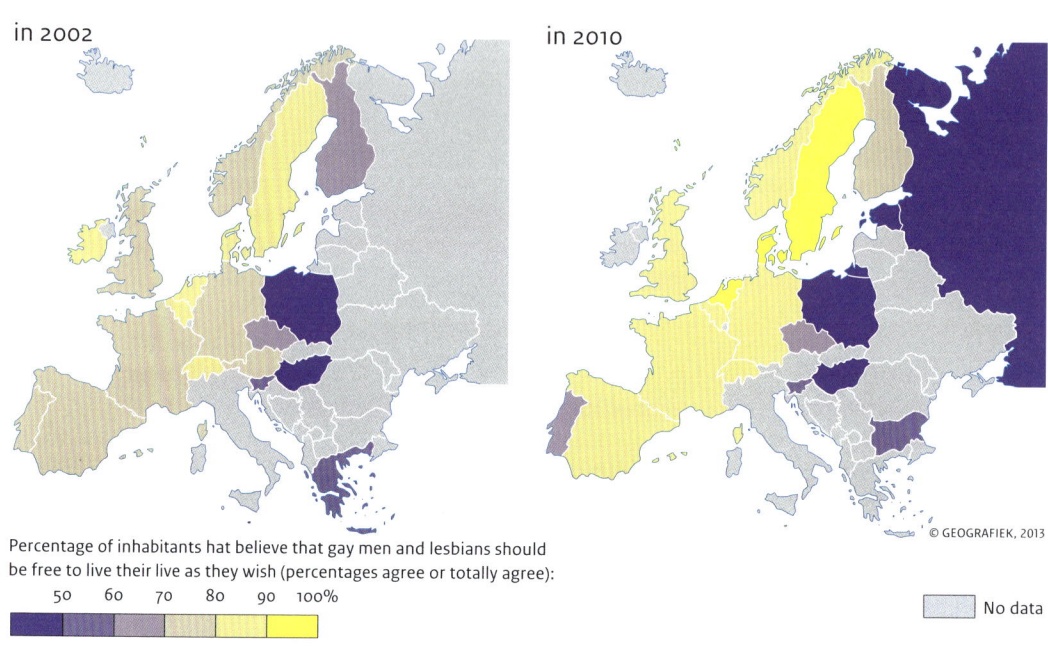

in 2002

in 2010

© GEOGRAFIEK, 2013

Percentage of inhabitants hat believe that gay men and lesbians should
be free to live their live as they wish (percentages agree or totally agree):

50   60   70   80   90   100%

No data

Source: ESS '02, '10

2.3   Summary

Over the last 30 years, all participating European countries have become more tolerant. On average, the level of tolerance increases by 11 percentage points every nine
years. Looking at the EVS data, the biggest change in attitudes took place between 1990
and 1999. However, the pace and consistency of the change vary considerably between
countries. As regards the pace of change, the Slovak Republic and Spain stand out for the
rapid increase in tolerance. Countries where the rate of change is notably slower, and
where the lack of change cannot be explained by ceiling effects due to relatively tolerant
attitudes, are Romania, Slovenia and Hungary. However, whilst changing more slowly,
Romania does exhibit consistency in the change in attitudes towards more tolerance
based on the measures for justification and homosexual neighbours in each period studied. Other countries showing a consistent trend towards tolerance are Iceland, Belgium,
France, Ireland and Spain.

No country became consistently more intolerant or stayed at the same level of tolerance between 1981/1990 and 2008. However, several countries seem to have undergone a change in attitudes in the 1990s but were unable to sustain this increase in tolerance into the new millennium, a finding in the EVS data which is supported by ESS data showing that many countries show no consistent or substantial increase in tolerance between 2002 and 2010. In some countries, such as the Netherlands, the lack of change is probably due to the already high levels of acceptance reached in earlier decades, leaving less scope for progress in the new millennium. In many other countries, however, attitudes remained stuck at a relatively intolerant level.

The pace of change, the consistency of change and the starting position of European countries in the 1980s and 90s set the scene for attitudes towards homosexuality today. In this sense, countries with relatively tolerant attitudes (countries where a fifth of the population or less think homosexuality can never be justified and regard homosexuals as unwanted neighbours, and where more than three-quarters believe that gay men and lesbians should be free to live their own lives as they wish) are Iceland, Norway, Sweden, Finland, Denmark, the Netherlands, Belgium, Germany, France and Spain. Countries in which between a fifth and a third of the population do not think homosexuality can ever be justified and/or would not want to live next door to a homosexual person, and where a majority believe that gay men and lesbians should be free to live their lives as they wish (though this latter attitude is less clear) are Great Britain, Ireland, Northern Ireland, Austria, Czech Republic, Slovak Republic, Portugal and Italy. Slovenia and Malta are countries where between a third and a half of the population believe homosexuality can never be justified and/or would not want a homosexual living next door. Countries where a majority think homosexuality can never be justified, would not want to live next door to a homosexual individual and do not agree that gay men and lesbians should be free to live their own lives as they wish are Poland, Bulgaria, Romania, Hungary, Estonia, Latvia, Lithuania, Russia and Ukraine.[12]

3   Gender and LGB: hand in hand?

Social acceptance of LGB individuals seems rooted in a broader gender belief system that focuses on appropriate pathways and roles for women and men in society. Policies also often focus on gender and sexual orientation and merge these issues together. In the Netherlands, for example, the government department that deals with equality and emancipation issues published its latest policy paper under the heading 'LGBT and Gender Equality Policy Plan of the Netherlands 2011 – 2015', addressing both inequalities based on gender and sexual orientation in the same policy plan. Also other countries merge their gender and sexual orientation policies.

It is not only policymakers who conflate gender issues and attitudes to homosexuality. Empirical studies in several countries (see e.g. Hooghe and Meeusen 2012; McVeigh and Diaz 2009; Nierman et al. 2007) or at European level (Takács and Szalma 2011) show a relationship between traditional attitudes on gender roles and intolerant attitudes regarding homosexuality. For example, a study by Nierman et al. (2007) compared attitudes to gay men and lesbian women among American and Chilean students. They found that the Chilean students reported more negative attitudes to homosexual men and women than the American students, and that this was (partly) due to more conservative gender role beliefs amongst Chilean students compared to their American counterparts. The study by Hooghe and Meeusen (2012) surveyed a sample of Belgian adolescents at the age of 16, and again when the respondents were 18 and 21 years old. They concluded that a traditional view of gender roles was strongly related to attitudes towards homosexuality, and those adolescents who became more conservative in their gender viewpoints reported accompanying increases in negative attitudes regarding homosexuality.

This chapter examines the relationship between attitudes towards homosexuality, gender role beliefs, and macro-level gender equality indicators. If this relationship exists, it would provide support for the merging of policies and point to important factor in determining attitudes towards homosexuality. Using EVS data from 2008, questions are addressed such as to what degree traditional gender beliefs go hand in hand with intolerant attitudes towards homosexuality in various countries, and whether citizens of countries that are conceived as feminine countries or countries with gender equality report relatively tolerant attitudes towards homosexuality.

3.1   Attitudes towards homosexuality and gender roles

One way to examine the relationship between attitudes towards gender roles and homosexuality is to examine correlations. A correlation is a single number that indicates the degree to which two aspects are related to each other.[13] The analyses for this section examine the correlation between a measure ('factor') that is based on six questions regarding women and paid employment and a measure based on two items regarding homosexuality.[14] Since only the data collected in 2008 were used, more countries could be included in these analyses than could be included in the analyses in chapter 2.

Figure 3.1

Relationship between attitudes towards gender roles and attitudes towards homosexuality[a]

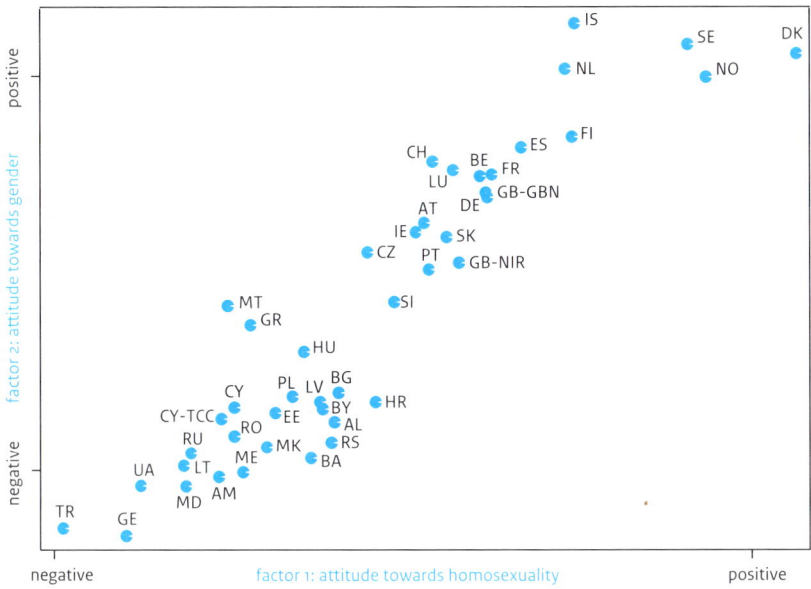

a   See Appendix B for a list of country abbreviations.

Source: EVS '08

A strong correlation (r = .56) was found at country level between average attitudes towards gender roles and average attitudes towards homosexuality indicating that countries in which people hold traditional beliefs about the appropriate role of women in households and working situations less often consider homosexuality justifiable and more often cite homosexual individuals as unwanted neighbours. Countries with intolerant attitudes towards homosexuality and conservative attitudes towards gender roles are clustered in the lower left corner of figure 3.1. Examples of such countries are Turkey, Greece, Russian Federation and Lithuania. The opposite (upper right) sector of figure 3.1, contains countries with tolerant attitudes on homosexuality and liberal attitudes on gender roles, such as Sweden, Norway, Denmark, Iceland and the Netherlands. The remaining countries are situated between these two corners. For example, countries such as Portugal, Austria and Slovak Republic, which report average attitudes on gender roles and homosexuality, are found in the middle area of the figure. No outliers were found such as countries which combine strong negative attitudes towards homosexuality with liberal attitudes towards gender roles or vice versa.

3.2 Attitudes towards homosexuality and the Gender Equality Index

There are several measures which are used to portray inequalities in the participation of women in society, such as gaps in education, jobs, power and health. For the present study, the Gender Equality Index (GEI) compiled by Social Watch was selected to examine the associations with attitudes towards homosexuality.[15] The GEI is based on gender inequity indicators in three dimensions: education (gender gaps in enrolment at all levels and in literacy), economic participation (gender gaps in income and employment) and empowerment (gender gaps in highly qualified jobs, parliament and senior executive positions). Scores are calculated on a scale from 0 (e.g. where no woman has a job or an income) to 100 (e.g. perfect equality in job and income distribution).

Figure 3.2
Relationship between justification of homosexuality and Gender Equality Index, 2008[a]

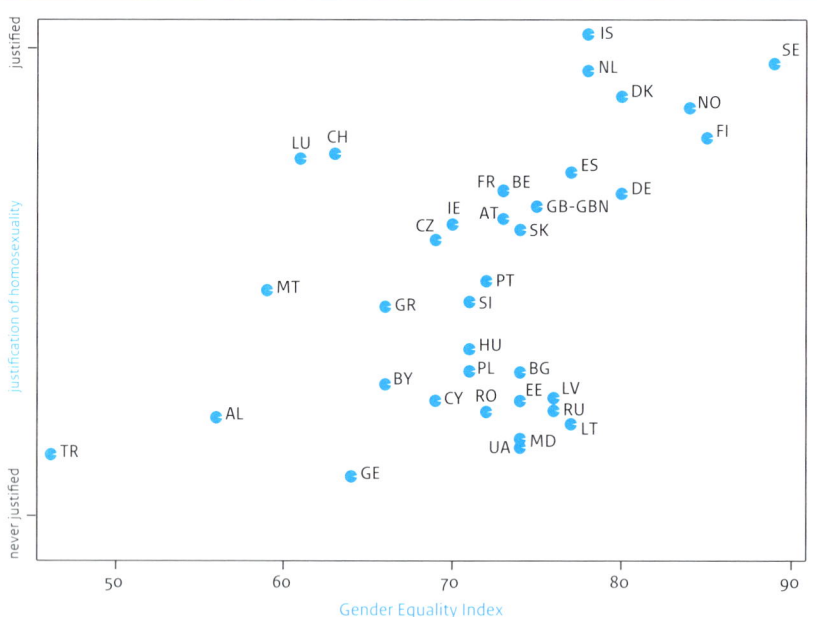

a   See Appendix A for a list of country abbreviations.

Source: EVS'08; Social Watch[16]

There is a relationship between a country's average attitude towards homosexuality and the GEI. The GEI shows a medium to strong relationship with average country-level attitudes regarding the justifiability of homosexuality ($r = .47$) and with attitudes to homosexual neighbours ($r = -.49$). In countries where women and men are more equal in terms of education, economic participation and empowerment, public opinion on homosexuality is more tolerant. For example, as illustrated in figure 3.2, countries with relatively high equality of women and men (as indicated by a GEI score of around 80 or higher) all report high scores on justification of homosexuality. An example of such a country is Sweden, with a GEI score of 89 and 12% reporting that they believe homosexuality can never be justified (7% of the population indicated that they would not want homosexual people as neighbours). Following these countries with relatively high levels of gender equality and tolerant attitudes to homosexuality is a group of countries reporting average attitudes to homosexuality and somewhat lower GEI scores (ranging from 70 to 75). An example of these countries is Austria (25% think homosexuality can never be justified, 24% want no homosexual neighbours, GEI score 73). The association between a relatively low GEI score and intolerant attitudes holds true for Turkey, Albania, Azerbaijan and Greece. For example, the GEI score of Turkey is 45 and 84% of its population report that homosexuality can never be justified. However, the association seems to be weaker for other countries with relatively low levels of acceptance of homosexuality such as Hungary, Poland, Bulgaria and the Baltic countries. Like the 'average attitude countries', these countries have GEI scores of between 70 and 75 (as high as 76 and 77, respectively, for Lithuania and Latvia), but report lower levels of acceptance of homosexuality (e.g. more than 50% of the population think homosexuality can never be justified). The association is also weaker in Luxembourg and Switzerland, which combine relatively low GEI scores (61 and 63, respectively) with relatively tolerant attitudes towards homosexuality (17% in Luxembourg and 20% in Switzerland indicate that homosexuality can never be justified).

3.3   Attitudes towards homosexuality and the masculinity/femininity dimension

When people are discussing societal gender issues, they often refer to the work of Hofstede. Hofstede analyzed the values of a sample of IBM employees recruited between 1967 and 1973 in a large number of countries. Based on his data, he constructed six cultural dimensions which are used to categorize cultures and societies. One of these dimensions is the masculinity/femininity dimension. Masculine societies are societies with a preference for achievement, competition, assertiveness, success and material rewards. Feminine societies stand for a focus on cooperation, consensus, modesty, caring for others and valuing quality of life above material goods. Masculinity and femininity together form two poles of one scale ranging from 0 (feminine societies) to 100 (masculine societies). Although this classification is not related to actual gender issues or gender gaps in society, the frequency with which these dimensions are used and the fact that they are often perceived as reflecting masculinity or femininity begs the question of whether they are related to attitudes towards homosexuality.

Figure 3.3

Relationship between justification of homosexuality and masculinity/femininity dimension[a]

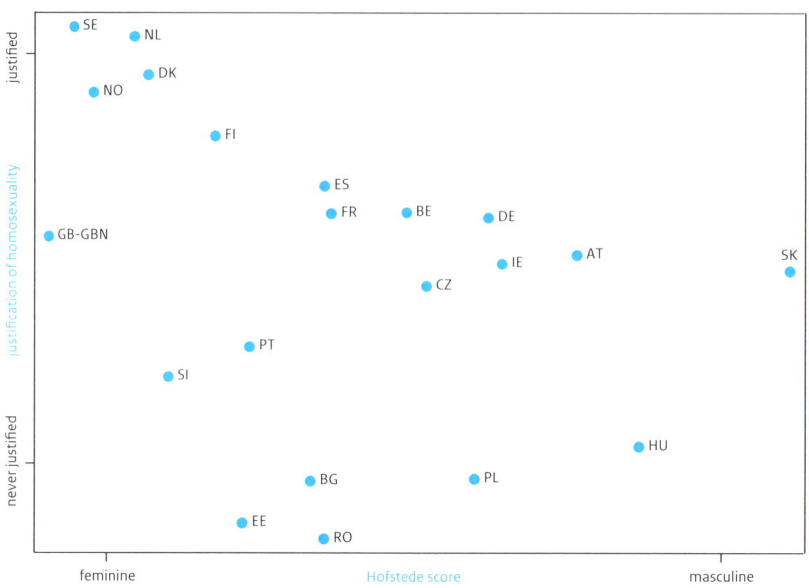

a   See Appendix A for a list of country abbreviations.

Source: EVS 2008; Geert Hofstede[17, 18]

In contrast to the results with GEI and gender attitudes, no relationship was found between Hofstede's masculinity/femininity dimensions and country-level attitudes towards homosexuality. There is a weak relationship between the attitude towards justification of homosexuality ($r = -.15$), and no relationship with not wanting homosexual people as neighbours ($r = .05$). The lack of a clear relationship between the two measures can also be seen in figure 3.3. In some countries, the culture is indeed feminine and attitudes are relatively tolerant. For example, Sweden, Norway, Denmark, the Netherlands and Finland are all feminine societies with high levels of tolerance. But Slovenia, Estonia, Romania and Portugal are also relatively feminine, and those countries do not have highly tolerant attitudes towards homosexuality. In Hungary, relatively high masculine scores do indeed go hand-in-hand with the country's relatively negative attitudes to homosexuality. But Austria, Switzerland, Ireland and Great Britain are also relatively masculine countries without accompanying negative attitudes on homosexuality.

3.4   Merging gender and LGB issues?

The current study confirms results from previous smaller-scale studies: attitudes towards gender and towards homosexuality are related. The way in which countries deal with gender issues is related to public opinion on homosexuality. A relationship was found on two aspects: a strong relationship with average attitudes towards gender roles in countries and a moderate relationship with a country's GEI score.[19]

To begin with the former, the our analyses showed that countries with liberal attitudes to gender roles also show a high level of tolerance of homosexuality. By contrast, in countries whose citizens believe that working mothers are not good for children, that women do not really want to work but would rather stay home, and that there is no value in achieving female independence through work, homosexuals are more often cited as unwanted neighbours and homosexuality is thought not to be justifiable. The analyses showed no exceptions to this rule (for example, a country with liberal gender attitudes but intolerant attitudes to homosexuality) and revealed that the relationship between attitudes towards gender roles and homosexuality was strong. Before jumping to conclusions, however, three critical comments need to be made in interpreting this finding. First, whilst it is in line with existing literature that traditional gender attitudes are related to attitudes towards homosexuality, it might also be the case that it is not the *gender* aspect but the *traditionality* of the attitudes that explains the strong interrelationship. It remains to be seen whether negative attitudes towards homosexuality are, for example, are also related to other traditional attitudes such as attitudes towards abortion and euthanasia.

The second critical comment is that it might also be argued that gender attitudes and attitudes towards homosexuality are manifestations of the same construct: a low tolerance of gender deviance. It has been argued that a negative attitude to homosexuality stems from a low tolerance of gender deviance and a preference for strict gender role adherence. In that sense, negative attitudes to homosexuality are negative attitudes towards gender (deviance). These attitudes are in other words one and the same thing and reflect whether or not people accept that not everyone adheres to prescribed traditional gender roles (e.g. women should raise children; people should love opposite-sex partners; women should not work outside the home; people should not have sex with same-sex partners; and so on). Whilst the current correlation of .56 between gender attitudes and attitudes towards homosexuality does not suggest that both attitudes are measuring the same thing, a broader operationalization of attitudes towards gender, including more sensitive measures concerning gender deviant behaviours or attitudes, should inform this line of reasoning.

The final critical comment is that attitudes to gender and attitudes to homosexuality might both be manifestations of the same underlying value orientations. An example of such an underlying orientation is post-materialism. Post-materialistic values are values in which quality of life, social issues and self-expression are considered important (Inglehart 1977). Liberal attitudes towards gender and homosexuality are then both specific expressions of a post-materialistic value orientation, and this could explain their relationship. It remains to be seen whether the relationship between attitudes towards gender and homosexuality remains after controlling for post-materialistic values. It is therefore important to assess the relevance of gender issues in a more elaborative framework, which also includes other factors such as value orientations. This issue is addressed in Chapter 4.

A moderate to strong relationship was found between a country's GEI score and public opinion on homosexuality. In countries with a high GEI score, i.e. countries with small gender gaps in education, literacy levels, income, employment and participation in highly qualified jobs such as a seat in parliament or a senior executive function, average attitudes towards homosexuality are relatively tolerant. However, the GEI is less predictive in Central/Eastern European countries where country-level attitudes to homosexuality are relatively intolerant but average GEI scores (compared to other European countries) were found.

One gender aspect that was not related to the attitudes towards homosexuality was the cultural dimension masculinity/femininity. A very low correlation was found with the masculinity index and attitudes towards homosexuality, and no clear picture emerged. There are indeed countries that are feminine and report high levels of tolerance, just as there are countries with high levels of masculinity and low levels of tolerance. However, there are also countries which are characterized as feminine but where public opinion about homosexuality is rather negative, and there are countries which are perceived as masculine but where relatively tolerant attitudes are found.

An explanation for the seemingly conflicting attitudes towards gender and GEI on the one hand and Hofstede's masculinity/femininity dimension on the other may be found in the 'genderlessness' of the Hofstede dimension. Hofstede used the labels 'masculine' and 'feminine' to characterize certain cultural aspects of societies such as achievement, assertiveness, modesty, caring for others, and so on. While these characteristics are often perceived as being male or female attributes, they are not related to gender aspects per se. In fact, one could argue that calling attributes such as achievement and assertiveness masculine and calling attributes such as modesty and caring for others feminine is a reflection of a traditional way of thinking about gender, rather than of 'masculine' or 'feminine' cultural dimensions of a society. In this sense, the masculinity/femininity dimension of Hofstede has little to do with gender.

4   Explaining differences

Differences between countries and shifts in attitudes towards homosexuality do no happen or exist in a social vacuum. They are intertwined with ongoing cultural, economic, demographic and political situations. Several studies have already investigated these influences empirically. Their titles illustrate the factors that have received attention: *Shaping attitudes about homosexuality: The role of religion and cultural context* (Adamczyk and Pitt 2009), *Cohort differences in tolerance of homosexuality* (Anderson and Fetner 2008a) or *Economic inequality and intolerance: Attitudes towards homosexuality in 35 democracies* (Anderson and Fetner 2008b). This chapter summarizes the factors that are associated with attitudes to homosexuality and have received empirical and theoretical support. Only studies comparing different places and/or times are included. After summarizing the existing literature on explanations for differences and shifts, we explore whether country differences in attitudes are related to factors reported in previous studies and gender measures based on multi-level analysis. We conduct the analyses using data from EVS 2008 and therefore focus only on differences between countries, not on differences over time.[20] While the overview of the literature, also provides explanations for differences between time intervals, therefore, the main research question focuses on explaining differences between countries.

The factors from the existing literature are grouped in three categories: social economics, religion, and policies and politics.

4.1   Social economics

Europe has undergone deep-rooted changes in economic, political and social life during recent decades, with different changes taking place in different countries in different periods. These changes affect people's attitudes to non-conventional groups such as LGB individuals. Modernization is a broad term covering various interrelated processes which all play a role in explaining differences in attitudes. Modernization processes that have received substantial empirical attention in relation to attitudes towards homosexuality are shifting value orientations in prosperous times, increasing urbanization, and rising levels of education. These processes receive empirical support in studies comparing various times and various places. For the sake of clarity, the modernization processes are discussed separately here, but in reality they are often interrelated (e.g. rising education levels lead to shifts in value orientations, etc.).

Value orientations and prosperity

One important aspect of modernization is increasing income and prosperity and decreasing levels of economic insecurity. Increasing levels of prosperity are related to shifts in general value orientations. Inglehart (1977) argued that as nations move towards more industrialization and modernization, people's value orientations change accordingly. Prosperity allows people to shift their attention from material concerns related to physical and economic security (such as food, shelter and safety) to post-materialist concerns related to quality of life, social issues and self-expression. This shift in concerns is accompanied by viewpoints that are more rational, tolerant and trusting of dissimilar others. Inglehart (1977) calls these value dimensions survival values versus self-expression values. Using data from the World Value Survey, Adamczyk and Pitt (2009) showed that greater endorsement of survival values rather than self-expression values was indeed associated with more disapproval of homosexuality. Gerhards (2010) and Hadler (2012) came to the same conclusion.

Prosperity and austerity

A relationship between prosperity and differences in attitudes towards homosexuality is also found in many other studies. Several studies show that tolerance is related to the income level of a country, to the income level of individuals, to unemployment status and to social class (Anderson and Fetner 2008a; Anderson and Fetner, 2008; Hadler 2012; McVeigh and Diaz 2009; Van den Akker et al. 2012; Stulhofer and Rimac 2009; Takács and Szalma 2011). Countries with lower income levels, individuals who earn less income, individuals who are unemployed and individuals who belong to the working class hold relatively negative attitudes to homosexuality. Interestingly, Anderson and Fetner (2008) conclude from their study of 35 Western democracies that income inequality within countries is a more important predictor of intolerance than economic development itself. While richer countries do indeed foster tolerance, not everyone is affected in the same way and those in a less secure position (such as working-class people and people with lower incomes) are more negative about homosexuality. Economic prosperity is related to attitudes towards homosexuality in the middle and upper classes, but not the working class. The authors conclude that both inequality across nations and inequality within nations are related to intolerance and that social tolerance is likely to be highest in rich societies where the benefits of economic prosperity are relatively equally distributed among all citizens.

Urbanization

Another aspect of modernization that is related to attitudes towards homosexuality is the degree of urbanization. In advanced modern societies, more people live in urban areas than in rural areas. Several studies have shown that people living in urban areas report more tolerant attitudes to homosexuality than people living in more rural areas (Anderson and Fetner, 2008b; Van den Akker et al. 2012; Anderson and Fetner 2008a; Van den Akker et al 2012; Stulhofer and Rimac 2009; Ohlander et al. 2005). Anderson and Fetner (2008) explained this by arguing that large city-dwellers more often perceive themselves to be part of a larger and more diverse world and have more contact with people who are dissimilar to them. People living in small towns, villages or the countryside are more often in contact with people similar to themselves and more involved in community issues. The lack of familiarity with outsider groups explains the finding that rural residents seem to be less tolerant towards LGB people. Interestingly, Takács and Szalma (2011) found a different result when examining data gathered in 2008 in 26 European countries: they reported the highest level of acceptance in suburbs of large cities, and the lowest levels among residents of large cities. They explain their findings by arguing that more LGB people live in suburbs and these areas seem to have developed more in the way of LGB infrastructure, while large cities have a higher concentration of immigrants who are known to hold relatively negative attitudes towards LGBs.

An explanation for the contradictory findings and lines of reasoning is that the relationship between attitudes and degree of urbanization depends on the national and local situation. For example, in countries with a strong LGB community which is concentrated in the areas surrounding the large cities, the line of reasoning taken by Takács and Szalma (2011) is valid, while in countries with low levels of LGB infrastructure (i.e. LGB bars, clubs or community centres) or a relatively intolerant population, the arguments put forward by Anderson and Fetner (2008) make more sense.

High levels of education

The final aspect of modernization that is frequently addressed in research seeking to get to the roots of negative attitudes towards homosexuality is education. Expansion of education is one of the key processes of modernization (Inglehart, 1977). Many studies have shown that increasing educational attainment over time or educational differences between countries are associated with greater acceptance of homosexuality (Anderson and Fetner, 2008b; Adamczyk and Pitt 2009; Van den Akker et al. 2012; Anderson and Fetner 2008a; Gerhards 2010; Hadler 2012; Loftus 2001; McVeigh and Diaz 2009; Ohlander et al. 2005; Takács and Szalma 2011). Ohlander et al. (2005) provide an overview of the ways in which educational levels influence attitudes towards homosexuality. Educational systems act as socializing agents, and attending school, college and/or university increases general knowledge, enhances critical thinking and expands people's frame of reference. This in turn induces tolerance of heterogeneity, new ideas or beliefs and non-conventional groups. Higher education also exposes people to different lifestyles and different norms and values from those they encounter at home. In addition, educational differences are reflected in what people watch or read, and this also influences differences in attitudes. Finally, universities offer a liberal environment and more opportunities to interact with LGB people.

To summarize, various assets of modernization and socioeconomic developments are related to attitudes towards homosexuality. When people's value orientations can be defined as post-materialistic, when levels of income are high and levels of unemployment low, when wealth is spread relatively evenly across countries, when people live in urban areas, and when educational levels are relatively high, more tolerant attitudes to homosexuality can be expected. These factors explain differences in attitudes between different times and places.

4.2   Religion

Religion is a frequently cited factor both in research and in the public debate on the 'causes' of negative attitudes towards homosexuality. Discussions about the relationship between religion and attitudes to homosexuality can often be summarized by stating that religious people are more disapproving of homosexuality than non-religious people. However, several nuances should be taken into consideration here. First, not every religious denomination holds the same negative viewpoints towards homosexuality. While most of the religious scriptures are not very supportive of same-sex sexual relations, denominations differ in the degree of literal interpretation of the scriptures, adherence to those scriptures and obedience in following their religious leaders (Adamczyk and Pitt 2009; Van den Akker et al. 2012). Several studies find differences in attitudes to homosexuality between different denominations. At global level, Adamczyk and Pitt (2009) showed that the attitudes of people with Protestant or Muslim religious affiliations are more negative than the attitudes of people with Catholic, Jewish, Hindu or Buddhist affiliations. In the European context, Van den Akker et al. (2012) showed that Muslim individuals disapproved of homosexuality the most. People with a Protestant or Eastern Orthodox religion disapprove of homosexuality more than non-religious people while, much to the surprise of Van den Akker et al. and contrary to other surveys, Catholic and Jewish people disapproved of homosexuality less than non-religious people. Gerhards (2010), using data from 2000 for the 27 EU member states and Turkey, showed that followers of Eastern Orthodox religions, Catholics and Muslims held more negative attitudes than Protestants. The diverging findings of these studies can be explained by differences in the reference groups used in the analyses (some studies compare religious individuals of various denominations with each other, while other studies compare religious and non-religious individuals) and differences between religions in various social contexts (e.g. Protestantism can be more or less conservative depending on the national context).

Other studies concerning the relationship between religion and attitudes towards homosexuality have shown that denomination is not the most important factor when trying to explain those attitudes, and that frequency of attendance at religious services has a bigger impact (Anderson and Fetner, 2008b; Van den Akker et al. 2012; Yang, 1997; Gerhards 2010). Religious people who attend religious services frequently hold less permissive attitudes to homosexuality, regardless of whether they attend churches, synagogues or mosques.

In addition to individual religious beliefs, Adamczyk and Pitt (2009) argue that the religious context of a nation influences individual attitudes towards homosexuality beyond an individual's own religious beliefs. For example, in countries with a strong dominant religion, the religious denomination also exerts an influence on culture, politics and the public debate. Therefore, people do not have to attend the religious services themselves in order to be influenced by the viewpoints of the dominant religion. Adamczyk and Pitt show that even people who are not personally religious are influenced by the religious tradition of the country in which they live. For example, people living in Muslim-majority countries or Protestant-majority countries are more disapproving of homosexuality than people living in Hindu, Buddhist or Catholic-majority countries, regardless of their own religious beliefs.

4.3 Policies and politics

LGB policies

As noted in chapter 1, laws, politics and attitudes are intertwined with each other, although it is not clear where the premises lie. Many studies have found a relationship between tolerant public attitudes and LGB equality and non-discrimination laws and policies (Lax and Phillips 2009; Loftus 2001; Riggle et al. 2010; Takács and Szalma 2011; Van den Akker et al. 2012). Takács and Szalma (2011) show that public attitudes are influenced by the introduction of legislation, with attitudes towards homosexuality improving after the introduction of LGB laws. Other authors argue that the way in which policies are designed and framed shapes the public discourse and opinions about certain issues (Bröer 2006). Lax and Phillips (2009) argue the other way around, and suggest that attitudes do not follow legislative introductions, but lead to changes in the law. Lax and Philips explored the level of public support that is necessary to achieve a 50% chance of changing certain policies or laws in the US. They showed that the amount of public support typically needed for a policy change depends on the specific issue at hand. For example, to have a 50% chance of policy adoption in the US, 50% public support would be needed in the case of same-sex relationships, but public support would need to be 75% to obtain a 50% chance of hate crime policies being introduced. Interestingly, they also show that the level of public support (as measured by public attitudes) greatly depends on the salience of the topic under consideration. For more salient issues, i.e. issues that are prominent in the public discourse, politicians will more often take public attitudes into account and laws will more often follow the majority preference. As Burnstein nicely summarized, the government is expected to do 'what the people want in those instances where the public cares enough about an issue to make its wishes known' (1981: 295, as noted by Lax and Phillips 2009). Lax and Phillips (2009) do indeed show, based on US opinion polls and policymaking, that roughly 57% support is needed on issues where salience is high and around 73% where salience is low. Another related factor is the existence of powerful conservative (religious) interest groups. When these groups are in place, policies are more related to conservative majorities and less to liberal ones. Conservative majorities are much more likely to obtain their desired outcomes, policies and laws. Whilst the study by Lax and Phillips is illustrative for the possible relationship between attitudes and policies, it remains in question whether the results hold true in other countries with different political configurations (i.e. political systems with multiple-party coalitions instead of the two-party system in the US).

Political systems and the EU

It is not only LGB laws and policies that are related to changes over time or differences between localities; broader national political systems also play a role. Anderson and Fetner (2008) report that in post-communist countries, public attitudes towards homosexuality are relatively negative. They note that this relationship is not simply explained by differences in economic development, since their analyses controlled for these factors. The explanation they offer is that due to their communist past, these countries might be more likely to have lower levels of social trust, a smaller LGB social movement, and a Church that plays a major role in the public sphere. This explains the relatively negative attitudes to non-conventional groups such as LGB individuals. Other authors have also shown a relationship between a state-socialist or communist past and more negative public opinion on homosexuality (Hadler 2012; Stulhofer and Rimac 2009; Takács and Szalma 2011).

Another aspect of the political system that Hadler (2012) showed to be related to increasingly tolerant attitudes towards homosexuality, using data from 1990-2010 for 32 European countries, is length of EU membership. His results show that intolerance of homosexual people decreases with increasing length of EU membership. He argues that EU membership is important because of the Copenhagen criteria stating that the rights of minorities must be respected in member states and candidate member states.

It is not only broad political systems and laws that are related to attitudes towards homosexuality; individual political viewpoints are also found to be related to those attitudes in studies that compare countries or times: right-wing authoritarianism and more conservative political values are associated with more negative attitudes (Van den Akker et al. 2012; Hadler 2012; Ohlander et al. 2005; Takács and Szalma 2011).

Civil and LGB movements

A further potentially important factor is the international linkage to the global civil society. A global network of governmental and nongovernmental organizations affects local attitudes and policies. The degree to which a country has internal linkage with these organizations focusing on human rights and minorities has an influence on social tolerance in that country. Hadler (2012) shows that intolerance of homosexual people does indeed decrease with increasing international linkage (especially with INGOs), but acknowledges that this could also be a bottom-up process: (I)NGO's might be more active in countries were relatively tolerant public attitudes make it possible to exist and take action.

It is not just linkage to global civil society that is important; the local or national LGB movement exerts an influence on public opinion on homosexuality as well. McVeigh and Diaz (2009) analyzed US data on voting to ban same-sex marriage and concluded that countries (states) in which at least one LGB organization is in place there is less opposition to same-sex marriage (the presence of general civil rights organizations did not exhibit this relationship). Adam et al. (1999) describe the development of local and national LGB movements in several countries. They describe the strategies used by the LGB movements, the goals pursued and the effect and success they achieved. Although there are similarities between countries, each country has its own country-specific path along which the LGB movement progresses and on which issues they focus. Several LGB movements have focused explicitly on changing public opinion – with greater or lesser success. Many factors are important in explaining the impact of LGB organizations.

In some countries these organizations are more or less forced to present themselves as a sexual minority, while in others they are part of a broad movement for human rights and equality. In the latter situation, changing the attitude towards homosexuality is part of a broader struggle or social movement.

4.4   Cohort replacement

Loftus reasoned that increasingly tolerant attitudes towards homosexuality are
explained by a changing 'demographic makeup' (2001: 762). When changes in demographic factors explain changes in attitudes, attitudes do not really change; the only
thing that changes is the makeup of a population, which simply contains more people
with demographic characteristics that are associated with more liberal attitudes. One
of the most frequently discussed factors in this regard is cohort replacement. It is often
argued that increasingly tolerant attitudes are due to the replacement of older, conservative generations with younger and more tolerant generations. Inglehart (1977) called this
'the silent revolution'. Indeed, many cross-national or time-series studies have shown
that people in older cohorts hold more negative attitudes to homosexuality (Adamczyk
and Pitt 2009; Anderson and Fetner 2008a; Van den Akker et al. 2012; Gerhards 2010;
Hadler 2012; McVeigh and Diaz 2009; Takács and Szalma 2011). In itself, however, cohort
replacement offers no explanation for why attitudes differ. The real explanations lie
mainly in the factors associated with cohort replacement: older birth cohorts grew up in
'less modern times', that is to say, in times when levels of prosperity were lower, survival
values were more important, people more often lived in rural areas, people had more
limited access to education, hierarchical religious denominations played a bigger role in
everyday life, many countries were not EU members, LGB organisations had little visibility, and so on. These processes and societal circumstances lead to less tolerant attitudes
towards homosexuality among older birth cohorts.
In addition, researchers have noted that the changes in the last 30 years in attitudes to
homosexuality have been too large and too rapid to be explained solely by the replacement of conservative cohorts. Several authors conclude that while differences between
cohorts do exist, changes are also taking place within all cohorts (Anderson and Fetner 2008b; De Graaf 2008),with attitudes becoming more tolerant over time within all
cohorts. Older generations have also shown a leap towards more tolerant attitudes to
homosexuality. It therefore seems that progress towards more tolerant attitudes or differences between countries cannot be explained simply by claiming that older, more
conservative cohorts are being replaced by younger, more tolerant ones.

4.4   Empirical test

In order to examine whether the factors that influence attitudes towards homosexuality
hold true in the EVS data 2008 and explain differences in attitudes between countries,
and also whether the gender indicators (see chapter 3) add additional explanations of
country-level differences, a multi-level analysis was performed. Multi-level analyses
explain differences in outcomes at country level and individual level simultaneously.
For example, multi-level analyses are used to examine whether differences in attitudes between people living in different countries are explained by income levels
in these countries or by the presence of a dominant religious denomination. Whilst
individual-level variables such as age are included, the focus of the current analysis lies
on country-level explanations. In other words: how much of the difference in attitudes

between people is explained by their country of residence, and can the factors studied offer explanations for this? Are there still differences in attitudes between people in different countries when factors such as social economics, modernization, religion, politics and gender issues are taken in account? Or are the differences in attitudes between citizens of different countries mainly explained by these factors?

Several individual measures were included in the analysis: gender, self-expression values, unemployment, income, urbanization, education, religious denomination, importance of religion, cohort, political orientation and gender attitudes. Country-level measures are gross domestic product (GDP) per capita, degree of income inequality within countries (GINI coefficient), presence of a dominant religion, communist past, length of EU membership and Gender Equality Index (GEI) score. The multilevel analysis was performed in seven steps, each adding a new cluster of variables to the model. Model 1 is the empty baseline model; Model 2 adds prosperity factors; Model 3 adds the modernization factors urbanization and education; Model 4 adds religious factors; Model 5 adds age; Model 6 adds political factors; and Model 7 adds gender issues.

Table 4.1

Multi-level analyses exploring justification of homosexuality in different European countries

factor	model 1	model 2	model 3	model 4	model 5	model 6	model 7
female (ref. male)		+	+	+	+	+	+
self-expression values (*ref.* materialist)							
mixed		+	+	+	+	+	+
post-materialist		+	+	+	+	+	+
unemployed (ref. employed)		+	+	+	+	+	+
income[a]		+	+	+	+	+	+
GDP per capita[b]		+	+	+	+	0	0
GINI[c]		-	-	-	-	-	-
urbanization[d]			+	+	+	+	+
education (ref. low)							
middle			+	+	+	+	+
high			+	+	+	+	+
religious denomination (ref. no denomination)							
free				-	-	-	-
muslim				-	-	-	-
orthodox				-	-	-	0
various				-	-	-	-
protestant				0	0	0	0
roman catholic				-	-	-	0

Table 4.1   (continued)

factor	model 1	model 2	model 3	model 4	model 5	model 6	model 7
importance religion[e]					+	+	+	+
religion country (ref. no majority)							
> 70% roman catholic				0	0	0	0
> 70% protestant				0	0	0	-
> 70% orthodox				0	0	0	0
> 70% no religion				-	-	0	0
age (ref. 15-24 years)							
25-34 years					0	0	0
35-44 years					-	-	-
45-54 years					-	-	-
54-65 years					-	-	-
> 65 years					-	-	-
political orientation[f]						-	-
communist past							
(ref. no communist past)						-	-
length of EU membership in years						0	0
attitude towards gender[g]							-
Gender Equality Index[h]							0
% unexplained variance at country level	28.8	7.2	7.7	7.0	7.9	5.3	2.8

Note. A + indicates a significant positive relationship between the factor and the attitude towards homosexuality; a - indicates a negative relationship and o indicates no significant relationship. The dependent variable is the attitude to justification of homosexuality; higher scores indicate more justification.
a   Higher scores indicate higher income
b   Higher GDP indicates more country-level income
c   Higher GINI indicates more income inequality within a country
d   Higher scores indicate more urbanized residential area
e   Higher scores indicate more importance attached to religion
f   Higher scores indicate more political affiliation with right wing
g   Higher scores indicate more conservative gender attitudes
h   Higher GEI score indicates more gender equality in education, economic participation and power

Source: EVS'08, Social Watch, United Nations Development Programme, Eurostat, European Union, CIA World Factbook

The multi-level analysis confirmed almost all the findings from the literature. The final model shows that more tolerant attitudes are related to gender (being a woman), more modern value orientations, having a job, higher levels of income, less income inequality within the country, more urbanized living areas, higher educational levels, considering religion less important, being younger than 35 years, having left-wing political orientations, and not having a communist past.

A few factors did not make a significant contribution to our model. Contrary to previous research findings, a country's GDP was found not to be related to attitudes towards homosexuality. This can be explained by the inclusion of the GINI coefficient. It has been argued that the degree of income inequality in a country (GINI) is more predictive of attitudes to homosexuality than the actual levels of income (GDP). Religious denomination also yielded different results from what was expected (Orthodox, Protestant, and Roman Catholic denominations do not report more negative attitudes to homosexuality than the category 'no religious denomination'). This can be explained by the inclusion of the importance of religion in the model, which has been suggested as being more important than the religious denomination as such. The lack of significance of macro-level religious influence could also be explained by including the importance attached to religion, or by the simplicity of the measure included in the model. Lastly, length of EU membership also made no significant contribution to the model.

Chapter 3 showed that attitudes to gender and GEI are related to country-level attitudes towards homosexuality when they are considered without taking other factors into account. The importance of assessing the relevance of gender issues in a more elaborative framework, which also included other factors such as modernization processes, was pointed out in the concluding section of chapter 3. The analysis performed here showed that attitudes to gender roles are also related to attitudes to homosexuality in a model that controls for other factors. However, GEI did not make a unique contribution to the model; the relationship between GEI and attitudes to homosexuality found in chapter 3 was explained by the relationship between GEI and other factors. Attitudes towards gender do explain some of the differences in attitudes towards homosexuality.

When looking at the explained variance in the different models at country level, the analysis shows that almost 29% of the differences in attitudes to homosexuality is explained by the country in which people live. The lion's share of the differences at country level is explained by factors included in the model. When controlling for differences in levels of prosperity (i.e. self-expression values, unemployment, income, GDP and GINI), only 7% of the differences in attitudes is still explained by the country in which people live. This percentage stays at around 7% when other modernization factors, religion, and age are included. The percentage drops to 5% when policies and politics (political orientation, communist past and length of EU membership) are included, and to 3% when gender issues (attitudes to gender roles and GEI) are fed into the model, thereby illustrating that these factors also explain additional variance in attitudes between countries. In the final model (Model 7) all factors included are taken in account. In this model, only 3% of the variation in attitudes towards homosexuality is still explained by the country in which people live. In other words, after including these factors and controlling for differences in factors such as modernization, religion, policies and politics and gender issues, differences in attitudes to homosexuality between countries become very small.[21]

4.5 Conclusion

A myriad of factors are related to changes in attitudes over time and differences between countries. Results of previous studies show that the rise of more tolerant attitudes towards homosexuality in Europe since 1981 that we noted in chapter 2 is partly explained by modernization processes, religious factors and policies and politics. Countries are moving from survival to self-expression concerns, cities are expanding rapidly, income and educational levels are rising, the (online) possibilities to link to the global civil society have increased greatly, the LGB movement is expanding enormously, strict adherence to organized religion is declining, communism and state-authoritarianism have been abolished, and many countries are (long-term) members of the EU. These processes are all related to progress towards more tolerant attitudes to homosexuality. Previous studies also show that modernization, religion and policies and politics explain differences between countries. The analyses presented here of differences in attitudes between countries in 2008 largely confirm these results and show the additional value of gender attitudes. When not controlling for any of the modernization, religious or political factors, 29% of the difference in attitudes is explained by the country in which participants live. This drops to 3% when those factors are taken in account.

5 Specific cases

Academics have conducted dazzling analyses to pinpoint the causes of shifts in attitudes towards homosexuality over time and differences between countries (see chapter 4). Many factors appear relevant when one is looking for answers to the question of why some countries are more tolerant than others. However, a question that remains unanswered is whether these factors can also shed light on why specific countries, which are quite similar in some aspects, have different public opinions on homosexuality.
To see whether the factors identified in chapter 4 are indeed capable of illuminating the differences between specific countries which were reported in chapter 2, four pairs of countries are discussed in this chapter. Pairs were selected in consultation with stakeholders whilst striving for a balance in terms of geography and attitudes. The countries selected for the pair-wise analyses should be close to each other in terms of geography, but dissimilar in terms of attitudes. The four pairs that were selected were the Netherlands vs. Germany, Poland vs. Czech Republic, Portugal vs. Spain and Latvia vs. Lithuania.
The pairs of countries were compared using Blinder-Oaxaca decomposition analyses. This analysis examines which part of a difference could be explained by the included factors. It also reveals the degree to which the included factors themselves contribute to the explanation. To give an example: Blinder-Oaxaca decomposition analyses demonstrate that 35% of the difference in attitudes between country A and B could be explained by factor X and Y, and 65% of the difference remains unexplained. Of the 35% of the difference that was explained, 10% was explained by factor X and 25% by factor Y. Findings of the decomposition analyses for the four selected pairs will be discussed in this chapter. In addition, tentative explanations based on existing literature will be sought for factors such as country-level factors (which cannot be included in decomposition analyses) that offer explanations for the unexplained part of the differences.

Figure 5.1

Decomposition analyses of differences in attitude to justification of homosexuality between pairs of countries[a]

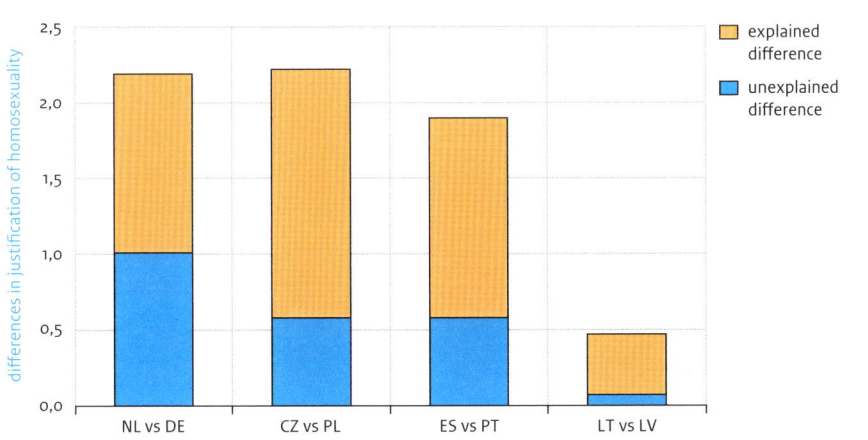

a   Explained and unexplained variances relate to the difference in country-level average attitudes
    towards the justification of homosexuality.
    The question in the EVS is: 'Please tell me for each of the following statements whether you think
    it can always be justified, never be justified, or something in between...[homosexuality]'. Answers
    were given on a 10-point scale (1 = never, 10 = always).
    Variables included in the analyses are age, education, income, unemployment, urbanization, reli-
    gious denomination, importance religion, post-materialistic values and attitudes to gender.

Source: EVS '08

Figure 5.1 shows that the differences in attitudes between the Netherlands and Germany,
and between the Czech Republic and Poland, are larger than the differences in attitudes between Spain and Portugal and between the two Baltic countries. Also, the
included variables explain a large part of the difference in attitudes between Latvia
and Lithuania, but a much smaller part of the difference between the Netherlands and
Germany. Figure 5.2 shows which variables explain the differences in attitudes between
the countries.

Figure 5.2

Decomposition analyses of differences in attitude to justification of homosexuality between pairs of countries[a]

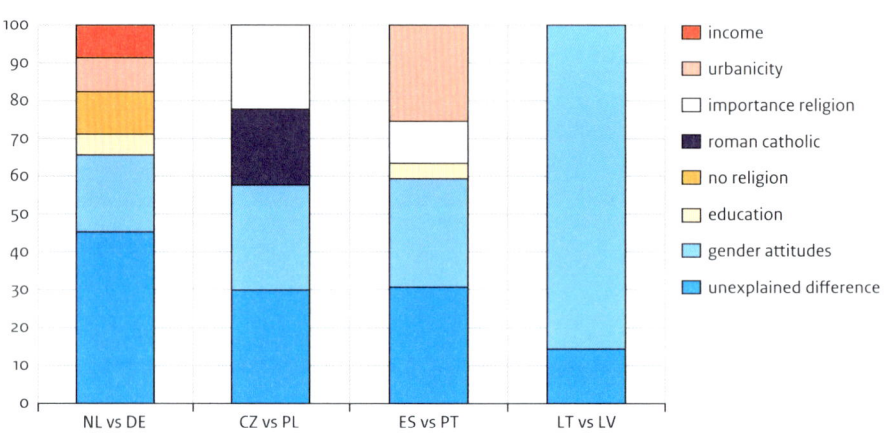

a   Explained and unexplained variances are expressed as percentages of the mean difference. For example, income levels explain 9% of the difference in attitudes towards homosexuality between Germany and the Netherlands.
    The question in the EVS is: 'Please tell me for each of the following statements whether you think it can always be justified, never be justified, or something in between...[homosexuality]'. Answers were given on a 10-point scale (1 = never, 10 = always).
    Variables included in the analyses are age, education, income, unemployment, urbanization, religious denomination, importance religion, post materialistic values and attitudes to gender. Only those variables that make a significant contribution to explaining the difference are included in the figure.

Source: EVS '08

5.1   The Netherlands versus Germany

Both countries report relatively tolerant attitudes towards homosexuality compared to many other European countries, but the Dutch attitude towards homosexuality is significantly more tolerant than the German attitude (Mean$_{NL}$ = 7.77, Mean$_{GE}$ = 5.57). Dutch individuals consider homosexuality more justifiable than German individuals. The factors that were included in the analyses together explain 54% of the differences in attitude. The factors that explained the difference were level of education, religious denomination, urbanization, income and attitudes to gender roles. The fact that Dutch citizens are more accepting of homosexuality is explained by the findings that the Dutch participants have higher educational levels, more often do not belong to a religious denomination, more often live in urban areas, have higher levels of income and hold more liberal attitudes to gender roles than their German counterparts.[22]

While 54% of the difference in attitudes was explained by the included variables, 46% of the difference was not. Apparently, these factors tell far from the whole story. Based on the literature review of macro-level factors that are related to differences in attitudes (and which cannot be included in Blinder-Oaxaca decomposition analyses), plus some qualitative reports of the situation and history of LGB citizens in the Netherlands and Germany, some tentative explanations can be offered:

— Germany was for a long time divided into two nations. The former German Democratic Republic had a communist regime and became a member of the EU after reunification in 1990. These factors are associated with more negative attitudes (chapter 4). One might think that this still resonates in different attitudes between Germans living in the former East and West Germany. However, analyses show that in 2008 there was no significant difference in attitudes between the two regions of the country ($F = 1.46$, $p = .23$).
— Sexual acts between consenting adults of the same sex were decriminalized in Germany much later than in the Netherlands. These acts were decriminalized in the German Democratic Republic in 1968, and in 1969 in the Federal Republic of Germany, but in the Netherlands this occurred as long ago as 1811 (after Holland was annexed by the French Empire and the *Code Pénal* came into force).
— Schuyf and Krouwel (1999) point to the role of the Dutch political culture, which is referred to as the 'politics of accommodation' (Lijphart 1968). Achieving consensus between various societal groups, all of which are minorities, has always been important in the 'pillarized' Dutch society.
— From the 1950s onwards, the Church was losing ground in the Netherlands. Both the Dutch Reformed Church and the Dutch Catholic Church developed and expressed more progressive attitudes, including on sexuality. Reformed and Catholic clergy played an important role in calling for the acceptance of LGB individuals (Bos 2010).
— According to Moeller (2010) the German LGB movement did not benefit much from the sexual revolution, which was framed as a heterosexual revolution. In the Netherlands, by contrast, the popular Dutch Society for Sexual Reform also advocated a change of attitudes towards homosexuality (Keuzenkamp and Bos 2007).
— In the 1960s and 70s, more and more popular public figures in the Netherlands came out as being gay. Homosexuality became more visible on television (for example in personality shows, soap operas and popular children's programmes) and in theatres.
— Religious denomination also plays a role at country level. Non-religious individuals living in countries with a religious majority are more negative towards homosexuality than non-religious individuals living in countries without a religious majority. Therefore, the higher number of Dutch inhabitants indicating that they do not belong to a religious denomination also influences Dutch attitudes towards homosexuality at country level. This is illustrated by the finding that German respondents not belonging to a religious denomination more often believe that homosexuality can never be justified (14.1%) than Dutch respondents who do not belong to a religious denomination (3.9%).

5.2   Czech Republic versus Poland

Public attitudes towards homosexuality are more tolerant in the Czech Republic than in Poland (Mean$_{cz}$ = 4.84, Mean$_{pl}$ = 2.62). The factors included in the analysis were able to explain the vast majority of the difference (74%). Three factors form part of this explanation: religious denomination, importance of religion and attitudes to gender roles. The relatively tolerant attitude of the Czech Republic can be explained by the fact that its citizens less often reported belonging to a Roman Catholic denomination; they also consider religion of lesser importance and report more liberal attitudes on gender roles. A quarter of the difference in attitudes towards homosexuality between the Czech Republic and Poland could not be explained by the included variables. Possible additional explanations are:

- The predominant Protestantism in the former Czechoslovakia was strongly individualistic and included respect for difference and dissent (Long 1999). Poland, on the other hand, had a much more family-oriented history. The Polish transition to democracy included a turn to 'natural' gender roles: a return to the traditional social roles of men and women was promoted by the former opponents of the communist regime and state policies today are very much pro-family (Keinz 2011). Homosexual individuals are portrayed as a threat to Polish family life, the pillar of the nation, and thus to Poland itself (Czarnecki 2007; Gruszczyska 2007).
- Civil society flourished in Czechoslovakia before the Second World War. The memory of that continued to influence Czech society over the years and has had a strong impact on the LGB movement (Long 1999). The first LGB organization, a professional counselling network, was founded in Czechoslovakia in 1988 (Lambda Prague). After the Velvet Revolution, the LGB movement expanded rapidly. The gay movement had links with the Civic Forum and members of parliament. In 1990 Jiri Hromada, head of Lambda Prague, ran as an openly gay candidate for Parliament. He was not successful, but he was very visible in the media and his campaign served as a catalyst for gay and lesbian involvement in politics (Long 1999).
- In Poland, several gay and lesbian organizations were launched (though still illegally) following operation 'Hyacinth'. From November 1985 to 1987, Polish communists had launched a campaign directed against homosexual individuals. Part of the campaign included police raids on bars, public baths and other places where gay men used to meet. This triggered the growth of an organized LGB movement in Poland. However, it was only after the fall of communism in Poland that LGB organizations were legally recognized – the first being the Lambda Groups' Association in 1990 (Szulc 2011). At first they mainly focused on community-based activities: offering a safe place to meet, providing counselling and support groups, etc. In 2003 the public advertising campaign 'Let Them See Us' (*Niech nas zobaczą*) marked a breakthrough in the visibility of LGB individuals. The campaign aimed to provide positive images of LGB individuals and to introduce the issue of sexual minority rights into the public discourse (Gruszczyska 2007). However, this growing visibility was met with strong resistance. Poland's accession to the European Union (in 2004) and the rise of nationalist, right-wing political forces fuelled homophobic sentiment further (see:

Gruszczyska 2007). In fact, LGB organizations were associated with the European integration process and paid a high price for it. "Their struggle was suddenly pictured as a
symptom of the bad influence of the EU on Polish society, and their goals as involving
threatening social models imported from the 'West'" (Chetaille 2011: 127).

— At first glance, the feminist movement in Poland seems less strong than in the Czech
Republic, and there has been less collaboration between Polish feminists and the
lesbian movement (Kowalska 2011). To what extent other coalitions between LGB and
other organisations were formed is not clear from the literature.

— The Czech Republic has a higher GPD per capita than Poland and a lower GINI index.
Higher levels of national income and lower levels of wealth inequality within a country are both related to more tolerant attitudes towards homosexuality.

— The vast majority of Polish people hold a Roman Catholic orientation and consider
religion much more important than citizens of the Czech Republic. In highly religious
countries, the Church has a wide influence on politics, culture and the social sphere
in the country and thus negatively influences attitudes to homosexuality, even among
individuals who are not themselves religious. This seems to be the case in these countries: while 23.5% of the Czech participants in the survey who do not belong to a religious denomination believe that homosexuality can never be justified, 38.5% of the
non-religious Polish respondents hold that opinion.

5.3   Spain versus Portugal

Spanish citizens more often consider homosexuality justifiable than Portuguese
citizens (Mean$_{ES}$ = 6.27, Mean$_{PT}$ = 4.38). A major part of this difference in attitudes can be
explained by the included variables (69%). The factors that made the biggest contribution to explaining the difference were attitudes towards gender roles, urbanization and
importance of religion. Spanish people are more accepting of homosexuality due to the
fact that they live in more urban areas, consider religion less important and hold more
liberal attitudes to gender roles. An additional, but minor, explanation is that the Spanish sample was more highly educated.

While a large part of the difference in attitude between Spain and Portugal was explained
by the factors included in the analysis, around a third of the differences is attributable to
other factors. Possible explanations may be found in the existing literature:

— Both Spain and Portugal have known a long period of dictatorship. The rule of the
Spanish president ended in 1975, with the death of General Franco. In 1978 a new
constitution was adopted under which all Spaniards acquired equal rights. Political
parties and trade unions were legalized and social movements emerged. During the
same period, LGB individuals began fighting for their rights (Llamas and Vila 1999).
In Portugal, the period dictatorship ended with the Carnation Revolution in 1974.
During the subsequent changes that took place in Portuguese society, there was no
very active and politically significant LGB movement. It was only after the emergence
of AIDS and in the context of NGOs set up to deal with the problem of AIDS that the
discussion of the specific needs of LGB individuals emerged in the 1980s (Carnero and
Menezes 2007).

- In Spain, there were many LGB organisations, which were also partly subsidized. After the withdrawal of public funding by the conservative Aznar government in the 1990s, LGB groups approached gay businesses to seek financial support. In exchange they promoted the gay scene. According to López Penedo (2012), this helped to articulate an open and very public LGB community. This increased visibility of LGB individuals coincided with a more positive presence of LGB characters on mainstream Spanish television (López Penedo 2012). This increased visibility might have contributed to the more tolerant attitude towards homosexuality in Spain.
- Spain has a higher GDP per capita than Portugal and a much lower GINI coefficient, factors which are both related to greater tolerance of homosexuality.
- Spain has a higher GEI score, which is also related to more tolerant attitudes towards homosexuality.

5.4 Latvia versus Lithuania

Both Latvia and Lithuania reported high levels of non-justifiability of homosexuality, but Lithuania reported higher levels of negative attitudes than Latvia (Mean$_{LT}$ = 2.42, Mean$_{LV}$ = 1.94). Some 83% of this difference could be explained, and only one factor played a role: attitudes towards gender roles. Most of the difference in attitudes between Latvia and Lithuania could be explained by the finding that people in Latvia hold more liberal attitudes to gender roles than in Lithuania. To provide an example, 29% of people in Latvia disagree with the statement that 'a job is OK, but what women really want is a home and children'. This figure is just 6% in Lithuania. Similarly, 47% of the population in Latvia consider 'being a housewife just as fulfilling as having a job', whereas in Lithuania 80% agree with that statement.

Around 15% of the difference in attitudes to homosexuality between Latvia and Lithuania could not be explained by the factors included in the analysis. Some tentative suggestions for additional relevant factors can be made, but since we could not locate any literature on this issue, those factors are based on suggestions provided by stakeholders[23]:

- Religion plays a more important role in Lithuania than in Latvia, with many Lithuanians being Roman Catholic and strictly adhering to the rulings of the Vatican. The EVS 2008 data confirm the dominance of Catholicism in Lithuania (79%) compared to Latvia (20%). In Latvia there is a mixture of Protestant, Catholic and Orthodox influences and therefore a lack of one predominant group that forces its line of thinking on society.
- Another contributory factor could be that Mozaika, the Latvian LGB organisation, has been relatively successful in raising the issue, increasing visibility and lobbying. The organisation is anchored in civil society and has ties with other organisations or networks. For example, the main funder of Mozaika (the Soros foundation in Latvia), has a high standing. The Lithuanian sister organisation (LGL) is struggling more to attain those goals.

5.5   Summary

Many factors that were reported in chapter 4 do indeed explain differences in attitudes between the Netherlands and Germany, between the Czech Republic and Poland, between Spain and Portugal and between Latvia and Lithuania. The majority of the differences could be attributed to differences in educational levels, income, religion, urbanization and attitudes towards gender roles. However, the portion of the difference that could be explained by the variables included in the analyses varied considerably between the country pairs, with 54% of the difference in attitudes between the Netherlands and Germany being explained, but 83% of the difference between Latvia and Lithuania. Also, not every difference in attitudes was explained by the same factors. For example, urbanization played an important role in explaining the relatively tolerant attitude of the Dutch (compared to the Germans) and the Spanish (compared to the Portuguese), but not in explaining differences between the Czechs and the Polish or between Latvians and Lithuanians. This shows that although the factors cited in the literature offer useful explanations, the explanatory power of specific factors depends on the social, historical and cultural legacy and structure of a given society – as is also illustrated by the role played by national historical events and the local LGB movement.

6   Conclusion

The preceding chapters have explored shifts in attitudes towards homosexuality, differences in attitudes between European countries and possible explanations for divergent attitudes. This chapter presents a number of summarizing, criticizing, and concluding comments.

6.1   Shifts in public attitudes

This study has shown that attitudes towards homosexuality are subject to change. Europe is becoming more tolerant. However, different countries are moving at a very different pace and from very different starting positions. While some countries were already relatively tolerant in the early 1980s and continued to develop even more tolerant attitudes (e.g. Sweden), others report relatively negative attitudes towards homosexuality and show no sign of increasing tolerance (e.g. Estonia). And there are also countries which reported relatively negative attitudes in the past but are a relatively tolerant society today (e.g. Spain). No country has reported a consistent trend towards more negative attitudes to homosexuality.

Changes have not taken place at a consistent pace since the 1980s. It seems that, in general, the biggest leap towards tolerance was made in the last decade of the previous millennium (1990-1999), after which changes came to an end or became much smaller in the first decade of the new millennium. This development is seen in relatively tolerant countries (where the lack of progress is partly explained by the fact that the already relatively high levels of tolerant leave less scope for progress), but also in relatively intolerant countries.

The pace and consistency of changes in attitudes combined with the starting position of European countries in the early 1980s shape today's picture of tolerance. Seen from this perspective, countries with tolerant attitudes are Iceland, Norway, Sweden, Finland, Denmark, the Netherlands, Belgium, Germany, France and Spain. Following these relatively tolerant countries are Great Britain, Ireland, Northern Ireland, Austria, Czech Republic, Slovak Republic, Portugal and Italy. And European countries that could currently be characterized as relatively intolerant are Poland, Slovenia, Malta, Bulgaria, Romania, Hungary, Estonia, Latvia, Lithuania, Russia and Ukraine.

6.2   Attitudes towards homosexuality and gender issues

The way in which countries deal with gender issues bears a moderate to strong relationship with public opinion on homosexuality. Liberal attitudes towards gender roles at country level go hand in hand with tolerant attitudes towards homosexuality. In countries where citizens hold liberal attitudes to women in areas such as work and bringing up children, they also consider homosexuality to be more justifiable and less often cite homosexual individuals as unwanted neighbours. As well as gender attitudes, societal gender gaps also play a role. A country's score on the Gender Equality Index (GEI) – which reflects gender gaps in education, literacy, income, employment and participation in highly qualified jobs such as senior executive functions or seats in parliament – is positively related to public opinion on homosexuality. Countries with smaller gender gaps in these societal domains report relatively tolerant attitudes towards homosexuality. One gender dimension was found to be unrelated to country-level tolerance of homosexuality, namely Hofstede's cultural dimension masculinity/femininity. No substantial correlation was found between the degree to which a country could be described as 'masculine' or 'feminine' and public opinion on homosexuality. As also discussed in chapter 3, this is related to the fact that Hofstede's masculine/feminine dimension has little to do with gender, but more with a traditional way of labelling societal characteristics such as achievement or caring for others as typically masculine or typically feminine.

6.3 Differences between countries explained: modernization, religion and politics

The rise of more tolerant attitudes towards homosexuality in Europe since 1981, and the variance in tolerance between European countries today, is explained by social economics, modernization processes, religious factors and policies and politics. The literature, and the analyses presented here show that countries are more tolerant when:
- people hold values that are more in line with self-expression than survival concerns;
- income levels are high and income inequality is low;
- cities expand and few people live in small rural communities;
- people attain high levels of education;
- strict adherence to organized religion is low and less importance is attached to religion;
- communism has been abolished;
- countries are (long-term) members of the EU;
- the (online) possibilities to link to global civil society are extensive;
- LGB movements exist, are strong and perhaps well connected to other organizations and movements.

The analyses in this study exploring differences in attitudes between countries in 2008 show that 29% of the difference in attitudes is explained by the country in which citizens live. After controlling for the factors modernization, religion, policies and politics and gender issues, the country of residence explains only 3% of the variation in attitudes. This shows that the factors included in the analyses explain the majority of the differences in attitudes between countries. It also shows that, in addition to the factors found in the literature, some of the gender issues that were explored in chapter 3 provided additional explanations for differences in attitudes to homosexuality between countries in 2008. When attitudes to gender roles were added to a model explaining attitudes to homosexuality based on modernization, religion and policies and politics. GEI did not provide an additional explanation.

Additional evidence of the usefulness of the factors in explaining levels of tolerance was found in the pair-wise country comparisons. Large parts of the differences in attitudes between the selected countries (the Netherlands versus Germany, Czech Republic versus

Poland, Spain versus Portugal and Latvia versus Lithuania) could be attributed to differences in educational levels, income, religion, urbanization and attitudes towards gender roles. However, the parts of the variance in attitudes that could be explained in previous studies and in the current pair-wise analyses differed considerably and never accounted fully for the differences in attitudes. In addition, not every difference in attitudes between countries was explained by the same factors. This shows that although the factors cited in the literature offer useful explanations, the explanatory power of specific factors depends on the social, historical and cultural legacy and structure of a given society.

6.4   Additional explanations

There is no single factor that determines attitudes towards homosexuality in a given country; attitudes are influenced by a myriad of factors. While many of these factors have been reviewed in this report, additional factors may also play a role which have not received attention in large-scale comparative studies and could therefore not be included in chapter 4. Four of these potential factors will be highlighted here: critical events, moral leadership, visibility and migration.

The trend analyses and literature review described here provide general explanations, but cannot take into account crucial events that occur in a single country or in a particular year. Countries can experience a 'critical moment' which draws massive media and political attention and leads to a shift in public attitudes (Pollock 1994). It has been suggested that this has happened in the us, where the brutal killing of a young gay man named Matthew Sheppard caused a stir in the media and in political circles (Brewer 2003). The same goes for the possible influence of 'elite signals', where important and influential key persons speak out on LGB issues and in so doing influence public opinion.

Another factor that might influence public opinion on homosexuality is moral leadership. Citizens base their opinions on how their moral leaders think about the issue. Examples of moral leaders are religious denominations or political parties. While the influence of religious denomination has been discussed and thoroughly examined in the literature, the role of political parties has received less attention. A study by Sherkat et al. (2011) illustrates the potential influence. The authors note that the resistance to equal rights for LGB individuals has become more vigorous in the Republican Party in the us during the last 20 years. Marriage equality has increasingly become a politically salient issue in the us, and the Republican Party has adopted an explicit profile as an opponent to such equality. Sherkat et al. (2011) show that in 1988, when marriage equality was a less prominent political issue, there were no differences in the support for marriage equality between Republicans, Democrats and Independents. In 2008, when marriage equality was a very topical en politically charged issue, Democrats and Independents were more supportive than the Republicans. It remains to be seen to what extent equal rights for LGBs will used by European politicians to give themselves a liberal or conservative profile, and whether this will influence the attitudes of their supporters.

The third important factor is the visibility of LGB people in the various countries. Knowing someone who is LGB is associated with a more tolerant stance on LGB issues. Therefore, in countries where LGBs are more visible (either in the real world or in the media), attitudes towards homosexuality might be more tolerant. The pair-wise country comparisons also suggest that visibility plays an important role in explaining public opinion on homosexuality, with political visibility (in the case of the Czech Republic), the presence of LGB characters in mainstream TV shows and soaps (Spain) and raising awareness of the issue (Latvia) being offered as possible explanations for the relatively tolerant attitudes compared to their comparison country (Poland, Portugal and Lithuania, respectively).

The final factor that is often discussed as a possible explanation for attitudes to homosexuality is migration. In countries with relatively high levels of acceptance, in particular, immigration from less tolerant regions is often perceived as a threat to the tolerance of homosexuality in the host country. While national studies show that migrants hold less permissive attitudes to homosexuality (for an example of a study on this issue in the Netherlands, see Huijnk and Dagevos 2012), it remains an open question whether differences in the influx of immigrant groups offers an additional explanation for differences in attitudes between European countries or over time.

6.5   Implications of the findings

Attitudes towards LGB individuals are not just a matter of private and individual opinions. Public attitudes play an important role in LGB citizens' everyday lives and partly determine how heterosexuals interact with LGBs. In addition, while the relationship between attitudes and policies or legislation depends to a large extent on the political structure of a country, varies between countries and changes over time, public opinions, laws and policies are interconnected. Public opinion on LGB issues is therefore an important element in fostering equality and anti-discrimination laws and policies. Attitudes to homosexuality are becoming more tolerant, thus creating opportunities to increase the equality of LGB and heterosexual individuals. Of course, attitudes are not sufficient in themselves to bring about equal rights and end discrimination. However, tolerant public attitudes do engender a climate that may be more receptive to ideas of LGB equality and non-discrimination. In this way public opinion in, say, the Slovak Republic, with more than half the population taking a positive stance on homosexuality, creates an attitudinal climate where the introduction of laws on recognising same-sex partnerships and same-sex parenting rights might stand a chance.

In addition, some studies suggest that different attitudinal climates require different approaches to enhance equality and non-discrimination. The work of Lax and Phillips (2009) and Helfer and Voeten (2013) shows that different social climates call for different advocacy approaches. For example, when the majority of the population supports the introduction of certain laws, it seems beneficial to try and make the issue at hand a salient political topic, since politicians follow public opinion on salient issues (Lax and Phillips 2009). By contrast, where the majority are not in favour of LGB equality and anti-discrimination laws and policies, a different approach will be more useful. Helfer and

Voeten (2013) show that rulings by the European Court of Human Rights (ECtHR) on LGB issues are related to increases in the probability of national policies being pursued in the Council of Europe member states. This is especially the case in countries with governments that are not strongly opposed to LGB issues, but where public opinion is relatively negative. In that case, the ECtHR rulings serve as a safe reference point for national courts and governments, and offer a more promising way of introducing LGB equality and anti-discrimination laws and policies. The introduction of new LGB policies and laws can in turn influence public opinion on these issues.

This study also has some implications for future research. First, this study was limited to the European context. Given the growing global attention for LGB issues, there is a need to examine the validity of certain claims (e.g. regarding shifts in attitudes and explanations for differences) outside the European region as well. The World Values Survey offers an opportunity for this.

Secondly, within Europe, it is important to broaden the scope of the research on attitudes by examining attitudes to specific groups within the LGB population (e.g. lesbian, gay, bisexual, and transgender individuals; see also section 6.6) and assessing a wider range of topics (e.g. attitudes towards LGB rights in addition to justifiability and having homosexual neighbours; see also section 6.6). The biennial European Social Survey (ESS) offers the best opportunity for this. The ESS is also the best gateway for exploring the idea that intolerant attitudes to homosexuality are a reflection of an underlying low tolerance of gender deviance (see also section 3.4). LGB individuals are often perceived as gender-nonconforming, and it might be a low tolerance of gender-incongruent behaviours which explains the negative attitude towards homosexuality. For example, a recent study by Keuzenkamp and Kuyper (2013) shows that the Dutch public are more negative in their attitudes towards 'masculine' women and 'feminine' men than towards gay men and lesbian women.

In addition, future studies should also try to examine the effects of the four additional potential explanations for differences in attitudes discussed in section 6.4. (critical events, moral leaders, visibility and immigration) and provide more insights into the interplay of attitudes, policies, politics, movements and change at local, national, and European level. Future studies should also address the shortcomings of the current study, as discussed in the next section.

6.6 Critical methodological comments

The EVS and ESS offer the most reliable, large-scale data sets available to track changes in attitudes to homosexuality across a wide range of countries. However, using existing data sets and conducting secondary analyses have the inherent drawback that the measurement of the issue at hand is not always as concise and elaborate as one would hope for. The measurement of attitudes to homosexuality has some unfortunate characteristics in the EVS and ESS. Drawbacks of the current measurements are the limited number of groups included, the restricted content of the items themselves and the odd location of the questions in the questionnaire.

To begin with the first drawback, the EVS items reflecting attitudes towards homosexuality use the terms 'homosexuality' and 'homosexuals'. Many people associate these terms with gay men, hence this leads to a limited measurement of attitudes to homosexuality in general (i.e. male and female homosexuality). The ESS does not have this limitation, since the item measuring attitudes to homosexuality is worded as 'gay men and lesbians'. Nowadays, however, academics, policymakers and national and international politicians and institutions do not use the term 'homosexuality' when addressing these issues, but speak of LGBT individuals: lesbian, gay, bisexual and transgender individuals. It is unfortunate that currently, no attention is paid to attitudes to bisexual and transgender individuals in the EVS or the ESS. The most recent Eurobarometer survey (2012) and several national studies (e.g. Keuzenkamp and Kuyper 2013; Kuyper 2012; Van Lisdonk and Kooiman 2012) provide good examples of measuring attitudes towards other groups in the LGBT community.

While understandable from the point of view that the EVS and the ESS have to cover many topics in just one questionnaire, from the perspective of comparing attitudes towards homosexuality it is unfortunate that those attitudes are only measured using one or two items that reflect a general attitude towards homosexuality. Other studies have shown that the attitude towards homosexuality is actually made up of several dimensions (e.g. Keuzenkamp and Kuyper 2013), and not all dimensions yield the same results. For example, while the general acceptance of homosexuality in the Netherlands is high, its social acceptance is limited in some cases. For example, while 13% of the Dutch population consider it offensive if a man and woman kiss each other in the street, this figure rises to 28% if the kissing couple are two women and to 41% if the kissing involves two men. Loftus (2001) also argues in favour of measuring several attitudinal dimensions by pointing out that people clearly distinguish between morality of homosexuality ('justification') and the rights of LGB people. While someone may consider homosexuality to be morally wrong (not justifiable), that person can at the same time be willing to support civil liberties and equal rights for LGB people based on the fact that they are a minority group. Questions on morality of homosexuality often tap into attitudes to sexual behaviour by LGBs, whereas questions about civil liberties relate to their minority group status.

The final drawback of the EVS data is the somewhat strange context in which attitudes towards homosexuality are surveyed. The item regarding the justifiability of homosexuality is included in a long line of issues which participants are asked to indicate whether or not they consider them justified. In addition to homosexuality, this list includes a number of moral issues such as abortion, divorce, euthanasia and the death penalty, as well as antisocial behaviours such as unlawfully claiming state benefits, cheating on tax, joyriding, lying and fare dodging on public transport. This curious context in which the item on homosexuality is located is quite likely to influence the responses of the participants. The same holds true for the attitude towards unwanted neighbours; as well as homosexual individuals, other examples of unwanted neighbours given include people with a criminal record and drug addicts.

6.7 Shifts in the future

It is impossible to say whether future attitudes towards homosexuality will become more tolerant, more intolerant or stay at their current level. Many factors would suggest an increase in tolerance in Europe. For example, educational levels are rising, the duration of democracy and EU membership is increasing, more attention has been devoted to LGB issues within the EU, and the global civil society and related movements are expanding. However, besides the fact that certain countries are not experiencing an increase in acceptance due to 'ceiling effects', at least two factors could halt progress towards more tolerance or even lead to diminishing levels of tolerance.

The first is the economic crisis that is currently holding Europe in its grip. With decreasing levels of income and increasing levels of unemployment and material insecurity, intolerance can rise. When a country is confronted with political or economic uncertainty, people turn their attention to basic needs and familiar traditional values, and hold more negative attitudes towards others who are dissimilar from them. Anderson and Fetner (2008) also warn against the possible backlash of certain economic events. For example, they argue that policies which have the primary aim of stimulating economic growth, but which also result in greater inequality, lead to increased levels of social anxiety and social distrust, which are then expressed in negative attitudes to minority groups such as LGB people.

Another reason to believe that attitudes to homosexuality might not increase in every European country is that globalization in general, and a more unified Europe in particular, could also lead to stronger adherence to local or national values. In a world that is becoming increasingly homogenized, people tend to attach more importance to their own local or national values and traditions. If this holds true for attitudes to homosexuality, it may be expected that in countries with a history of intolerance of homosexuality, no change will take place, or attitudes might even become more intolerant. Especially where tolerance of homosexuality is seen as something that is forced upon a country by the EU, strong anti-EU sentiments can spill over into intolerant attitudes towards LGB individuals among certain groups.

Whether the above push or the pull factors determining tolerance will have the greatest influence, and whether European countries will move towards more tolerant or more negative attitudes to homosexuality, will only become apparent when future data collections for the EVS and ESS become available.

Summary

Attitudes to homosexuality vary widely across Europe. While in one country thousands of LGB people and supportive heterosexuals take to the streets during gay pride events, in another country a similar number of people flock the streets to express their disapproval of homosexuality. Some European countries have opened the door to same-sex marriage, while in their neighbouring countries it is not possible to register relationships between people of the same sex. And where the discussion of homosexuality has been established as one of the attainment targets in some countries, other countries are introducing legislation to prohibit 'gay propaganda' in schools.

In addition to wide differences in the legal context, there are also differences in public attitudes to homosexuality. A recent survey by the European Commission (2012), for example, shows that only 2% of the population in Sweden say they would feel uncomfortable with the idea of the governmental leader in the country being lesbian, gay, or bisexual (LGB). In the Slovak Republic, by contrast, only 2% would feel comfortable with this.

Attitudes to homosexuality are more than mere individual opinions, but form part of the social and political structures which foster or hinder the equality and emancipation of LGB citizens.[1] Improving the social acceptance of homosexuality is accordingly one of the pillars of the Dutch government's emancipation policy. The Dutch Ministry of Education, Culture and Science is responsible for coordinating this policy, and it was consequently this Ministry which asked the Netherlands Institute for Social Research|scp to carry out a study of the international acceptance of homosexuality. In this report we provide answers to the following questions:

1 Which shifts in public attitudes towards homosexuality[2] can be found in European countries?
2 To what degree are gender issues related to attitudes towards homosexuality in Europe?
3 To what degree can differences in attitudes between European countries be explained by modernisation, religion and policies and politics?

The study draws on existing data from two large scale studies which facilitate comparisons of European countries over time: the European Values Study (EVS) and the European Social Survey (ESS). Both data sets contain questions on attitudes towards homosexuality, produce comparable data across more than twenty countries and have been repeated on several occasions (EVS: 1981, 1990, 1999 and 2008; ESS: 2002, 2004, 2006, 2008 en 2010). More information on the data sets may be found at www.scp.nl, www.europeansocialsurvey.org and www.europeanvaluesstudy.eu.

Changes in attitudes to homosexuality

The analyses show that the attitudes of the European population towards homosexuality are not set in stone. Europe has become more tolerant over the last 30 years. In all countries – without exception – acceptance is greater today than at the start of the 1980s.

Acceptance of homosexuality rose particularly strongly in the period between 1990 and 1999, following which the rate of increase in both relatively tolerant and relatively intolerant countries slackened off. There are however wide differences in the pace of the changes, their continuation and the starting positions of countries in the early 1980s. While some countries were already relatively tolerant in 1981 and also show a fairly consistent increase in acceptance (e.g. Sweden), there are also countries which were relatively intolerant in 1981/1990 and which show little movement towards more accept- ance (e.g. Estonia). In addition, there are countries which were relatively intolerant 30 years ago but which are now characterised by a high level of acceptance (e.g. Spain). The fastest and biggest changes have taken place in Spain and the Slovak Republic, while change has been most limited in Romania, Slovenia and Hungary.

Iceland, Norway, Sweden, Finland, Denmark, the Netherlands, Belgium, Germany, France and Spain were the most tolerant countries in 2008/2010. Less than a fifth of the population in these countries think that homosexuality can never be justified; less than a fifth cite homosexuals as people they would not want as neighbours; and more than three-quarters believe that gay men and lesbians should be allowed to live their lives as they wish. These countries are followed by a group of countries, made up of Great Britain, Ireland, Northern Ireland, Austria, Czech Republic, Slovak Republic, Portugal and Italy, where between a fifth and a third of the population believe that homosexual- ity can never be justified, would prefer not to have homosexual neighbours and where a smaller majority think that gay men and lesbians should be allowed to live their lives as they wish. Between a third and half the population of Slovenia and Malta would not want to live next door to a gay person and believe that homosexuality can never be justified. Finally, there is a group of countries where a broad majority of the population feel that homosexuality can never be justified, would not want homosexuals as neighbours and disagree with the statement that gay men and lesbians should be allowed to live their lives as they wish. This group comprises Poland, Bulgaria, Romania, Hungary, Estonia, Latvia, Lithuania, Russia and Ukraine.

Relationship with gender issues

The report looks at whether there is a relationship between attitudes towards homo- sexuality and a number of gender issues. First, the relationship between attitudes towards homosexuality and attitudes to the division of roles between men and women is investigated. These attitudes were found to be strongly associated: in countries where people hold more liberal views on gender roles, the acceptance of homosexuality is also greater. The study then examines whether the acceptance of homosexuality is related to the Gender Equality Index (GEI). This index reflects levels of gender inequality in educa- tion, economic participation and influence or power in a given country. Once again, a relationship is found: in countries where men and women are more equal in terms of education, economic participation and influence or power, the population takes a more positive stance on homosexuality. There are however exceptions to this. In the Baltic countries, for example, there is a relatively high degree of equality between men and women in the areas cited, but acceptance of homosexuality is limited. Finally, the relationship between the cultural dimension masculinity/femininity propounded by

Hofstede is examined. No relationship is found. This can perhaps be explained by the lack of 'gender' in Hofstede's dimension. Although the dimensions are described as 'masculine' and 'feminine', these terms refer only to characteristics of a country such as competitiveness or caring for others. Apart from the name, therefore, the dimension in reality has little to do with masculinity or femininity.

Differences explained

A number of factors emerge from the literature and our analyses which are associated with greater acceptance of homosexuality. A relatively tolerant attitude to homosexuality in a country is associated with:
– attaching more importance to post-materialistic values (e.g. attention for social issues or well-being) than to values related to physical and economic safety;
– higher incomes and smaller income differentials within a country;
– a more urbanised population;
– higher education levels;
– a population with a less dominant religious denomination and where organised religious gatherings are attended less frequently;
– more liberal views on the division of roles between men and women;
– the absence of a communist past;
– longer membership of the European Union (EU);
– stronger links to global civil society;
– a stronger LGB movement and, possibly, ties between that movement and other organisations or networks.

The above factors explain a very large part of the differences in acceptance of homosexuality between countries. It should however be noted that a more in-depth investigation of comparisons between specific pairs of countries (e.g. if Dutch and German attitudes to homosexuality are examined, or if Czechs and Poles are compared), there is still a large part of the differences which cannot be explained by differences in the factors cited above. Although the factors offer a good explanation, therefore, their explanatory power does depend on a country's social, historical and cultural context. Additional factors shown to be related to acceptance in the in-depth analyses included the local LGB movement, moral leadership by influential individuals and the visibility of homosexuality in society and the national media.

Qualifying comments

This report shows that Europe is on the way towards greater acceptance of homosexuality, but that there are still wide differences between countries in terms of their starting position, the magnitude of the change and the continuance of the trend. The report also looks at the fact that changes in attitudes to homosexuality do not take place in a social or historical vacuum, but are associated with broader modernisation processes (e.g. rising education levels), religious factors and political developments.
There are a number of limitations to this report. The data sets used are the most reliable currently available, but carry a number of drawbacks. For example, they contain only one

or two questions about homosexuality, making it impossible to determine accurately whether attitudes differ on different topics (e.g. attitudes towards same-sex marriage or parenting by same-sex couples). Moreover, the surveys contain no questions about the acceptance of specific groups. The questions are formulated in general terms and relate to homosexual men, and sometimes to lesbian women, but whether there are differences in the acceptance of these subgroups is not known. In addition, transgender and bisexual individuals are not mentioned at all in these surveys.

Recommendations

Public attitudes can influence political decision-making on the rights of LGB individuals. Different social climates demand a different approach in seeking to foster equal rights. Other recommendations relate to future research, which should take more account of the diversity within the target group (e.g. differences in attitudes towards lesbian women and gay men, attitudes to transgender and bisexual individuals) and which should investigate what role rejection of gender-nonconformity plays in negative attitudes to homosexuality.

Tolerance in the future

Whether Europe will become more tolerant in the future remains to be seen. On the one hand there are reasons to assume that the acceptance of homosexuality will increase further: average education levels are rising, fewer and fewer people live in small rural communities, the length of EU membership is increasing and the opportunities for linking (including online) to global civil society and LGB movements are increasing rapidly. There are also several European countries, institutions and regulations which argue for more equality for LGB citizens in Europe. These factors could contribute to a further increase in the acceptance of homosexuality.

At the same time, however, there are at least two important reasons for not assuming that it is certain that social acceptance of homosexuality will increase everywhere. First, the economic crisis is holding Europe firmly in its grip. Unemployment is rising, incomes are falling and – depending on the policy pursued – income differentials are widening. These are factors that are associated with less social acceptance. When a country is going through difficult political or economic times, people are inclined to turn to traditional values which offer certainty and to focus on their physical and economic needs. This often takes place at the expense of a tolerant attitude to minorities, including lesbian, gay, bisexual and transgender individuals.

The second reason for questioning whether the acceptance of homosexuality will continue to increase is the phenomenon that in an increasingly globalising world, people often wish to protect local and national customs. People seek to hold onto traditions and values that they regard as an intrinsic part of their own country, while issues that are perceived as being 'imposed by Europe' are rejected. If this process also occurs with regard to the acceptance of homosexuality, it may be that countries with negative attitudes in past and present will continue to hold on to this intolerance. Anti-EU sentiment could even turn attitudes more negative within certain groups.

Dutch Summary (Nederlandse Samenvatting)

In Europa bestaan grote verschillen in de omgang met homoseksualiteit. Waar in het ene land duizenden homoseksuelen en solidaire heteroseksuelen op de been zijn tijdens gay prides, is in het andere land eenzelfde hoeveelheid mensen op de been om hun afkeur van homoseksualiteit te uiten. Sommige Europese landen hebben het burgerlijk huwelijk opengesteld voor paren van gelijk geslacht, terwijl in hun buurlanden registratie van relaties tussen personen van gelijk geslacht niet mogelijk is. En waar in Nederland het bespreken van homoseksualiteit sinds eind 2012 in de kerndoelen van het onderwijs staat, voeren andere landen juist wetgeving in om 'homo- propaganda' op scholen te verbieden.

Naast grote verschillen in de wettelijke context zijn er verschillen in de houding van de bevolking ten opzichte van homoseksualiteit. Zo laat een recent onderzoek van de Europese Commissie (2012) zien dat in Zweden slechts 2% van de bevolking aangeeft zich *on*comfortabel te voelen bij het idee dat de hoogste leider in het land lesbisch, homoseksueel of biseksueel (LHB) zou zijn. In Slowakije zou slechts 2% zich hier comfortabel bij voelen.

Attituden ten opzichte van homoseksualiteit zijn meer dan slechts individuele opvattingen, zij vormen een onderdeel van maatschappelijke en politieke structuren die gelijkheid en emancipatie van LHB burgers bevorderen of belemmeren. Het bevorderen van de sociale acceptatie van homoseksualiteit vormt dan ook een van de peilers van het emancipatiebeleid van de Nederlandse regering. Het ministerie van Onderwijs, Cultuur en Wetenschap (OCW)coördineert dit beleid. Vanuit dit ministerie kwam dan ook de vraag aan het Sociaal en Cultureel Planbureau (SCP) om onderzoek te doen naar de internationale acceptatie van homoseksualiteit. In dit rapport geven wij antwoord op de volgende vragen:

1 Welke veranderingen in de houding ten opzichte van homoseksualiteit vinden er plaats in Europa?
2 In hoeverre hangt de houding ten opzichte van homoseksualiteit samen met de omgang met gender issues in Europese landen?
3 In hoeverre vallen verschillen in homoacceptatie tussen landen toe te schrijven aan andere verschillen tussen landen zoals verschillen in modernisering, religie en politiek?

Het onderzoek maakt gebruik van bestaande data uit grootschalige studies die vergelijkingen tussen Europese landen door de tijd heen mogelijk maken: de European Values Study (EVS) en de European Social Survey (ESS). Beide datasets bevatten vragen over de houding ten opzichte van homoseksualiteit, vergelijkbare gegevens voor meer dan twintig landen en zijn herhaaldelijk uitgevoerd (EVS: 1981, 1990, 1999 en 2008; ESS: 2002, 2004, 2006, 2008 en 2010). Meer informatie over de datasets is te vinden op www.scp.nl, www.europeansocialsurvey.org en www.europeanvaluesstudy.eu.

Veranderingen in houding ten opzichte van homoseksualiteit

De analyses laten zien dat de houding van de Europese bevolking ten opzichte van homoseksualiteit niet in steen gebeiteld is. Gedurende de afgelopen 30 jaar is Europa toleranter geworden. In alle landen – zonder uitzondering – is de acceptatie op dit moment groter dan begin jaren tachtig. Met name in de periode tussen 1990 en 1999 nam in veel landen de acceptatie van homoseksualiteit toe. Daarna zwakte de toename in zowel relatief tolerante als relatief intolerante landen af. Er zijn echter grote onderlinge verschillen in het tempo van de veranderingen, het doorzetten van veranderingen en de uitgangsposities van landen begin jaren tachtig. Terwijl er landen zijn die in 1981 al relatief tolerant waren en daar bovenop een vrij consistente toename van acceptatie laten zien (bijv. Zweden), zijn er ook landen die in 1981/1990 relatief intolerant waren en die weinig beweging naar meer acceptatie laten zien (bijv. Estland) en landen die 30 jaar geleden relatief intolerant waren, maar nu een hoog niveau van acceptatie kennen (bijv. Spanje). De snelste en grootste veranderingen hebben plaatsgevonden in Spanje en Slowakije, terwijl verandering het meest beperkt was in Roemenië, Slovenië en Hongarije. IJsland, Noorwegen, Zweden, Finland, Denemarken, Nederland, België, Duitsland, Frankrijk en Spanje zijn in 2008/2010 het meest tolerant. In deze landen vindt minder dan een vijfde van de bevolking homoseksualiteit nooit gerechtvaardigd, beschouwt minder dan een vijfde homoseksuelen als ongewenste buren en vindt meer dan driekwart dat homoseksuele mannen en lesbische vrouwen vrij moeten zijn om hun leven te leiden zoals zij dat zelf willen. Daarna volgt de groep landen waar een vijfde tot een derde homoseksualiteit nooit gerechtvaardigd vindt, liever geen homoseksuele buren heeft en een krappere meerderheid vindt dat homoseksuele mannen en lesbische vrouwen vrij moeten zijn om hun eigen leven te leiden: Groot Brittannië, Ierland, Noord Ierland, Oostenrijk, Tsjechië, Slowakije, Portugal en Italië. Vervolgens wil een derde tot de helft van de Sloveense en Maltese bevolking niet naast een homo wonen en vinden zij homoseksualiteit niet gerechtvaardigd. Als laatste is er een groep landen waarin, grofweg, de meerderheid van de bevolking vindt dat homoseksualiteit nooit te rechtvaardigen valt, homoseksuelen ongewenst zijn als buren en ook de meerderheid het niet eens is met de stelling dat deze groep vrij moet zijn om te leven zoals zij zelf willen. Deze groep bestaat uit Polen, Bulgarije, Roemenië, Hongarije, Estland, Letland, Litouwen, Rusland en Oekraïne.

Samenhang met gender issues

In het rapport is gekeken of de houding ten opzichte van homoseksualiteit samenhangt met verschillende gender issues. Allereerst werd de samenhang tussen de houding ten opzichte van homoseksualiteit en de houding ten opzichte van de taakverdeling tussen mannen en vrouwen onderzocht. Deze bleken sterk met elkaar samen te hangen. In landen waar men vrijere opvattingen heeft over de taakverdeling is de acceptatie van homoseksualiteit ook groter. Vervolgens werd onderzocht of de acceptatie van homoseksualiteit gerelateerd was aan de Gender Equality Index (GEI). Deze maat geeft de sekseongelijkheid in opleiding, economische participatie en invloed of macht in een land weer. Ook hier werd een verband gevonden: landen waarin beide seksen meer gelijk zijn met betrekking tot opleiding, economische participatie en invloed of macht, staat de bevolking positiever ten opzichte van homoseksualiteit. Hierop zijn echter wel uitzonderingen. Zo is er in de Baltische landen een relatief grote gelijkheid tussen mannen en vrouwen op de genoemde gebieden, maar is de acceptatie van homoseksualiteit beperkt. Tot slot werd de samenhang tussen de cultuurdimensie mannelijkheid/vrouwelijkheid van Hofstede onderzocht. Hier werd geen relatie mee gevonden. Dit kan wellicht worden verklaard door het gebrek aan 'gender' in Hofstede's dimensie. De dimensie heten 'mannelijk' en 'vrouwelijk', maar daar worden slechts eigenschappen als competentiegerichtheid of zorgzaamheid mee bedoeld. Naast de naam lijkt de dimensie dus eigenlijk weinig met mannelijkheid of vrouwelijkheid van doen te hebben.

Verschillen verklaard

Uit de literatuur en onze analyses komen een aantal factoren voor die samengaan met meer acceptatie van homoseksualiteit. Een relatief tolerante houding ten opzichte van homoseksualiteit in een land hangt samen met:

– het hechten van een groter belang aan postmaterialistische waarden (bijv. aandacht voor sociale kwesties of welzijn) dan aan waarden die te maken hebben met fysieke en economische veiligheid;
– hogere inkomens en kleinere inkomensverschillen binnen een land;
– een meer stedelijk wonende bevolking;
– een hoger opleidingsniveau;
– een bevolking die zich minder tot een bepaalde religieuze stroming rekent en minder frequent georganiseerde religieuze bijeenkomsten bezoekt;
– vrijere opvattingen over de taakverdeling tussen mannen en vrouwen;
– de afwezigheid van een communistisch verleden;
– een langduriger lidmaatschap van de Europese Unie (EU);
– sterkere banden met de 'global civil society';
– een sterkere homobeweging en de verbondenheid hiervan met andere organisaties of netwerken.

De bovengenoemde factoren verklaren een zeer groot deel van de verschillen in acceptatie van homoseksualiteit tussen landen. Wel moet worden opgemerkt dat als er dieper wordt ingegaan op paarsgewijze vergelijkingen tussen specifieke landen (bijv. als de Nederland houding en de Duitse houding ten opzichte van homoseksualiteit onder de loep worden genomen, of de Tsjechische en de Poolse met elkaar worden vergeleken), dat er dan ook nog een groot deel van de verschillen niet door verschillen in bovengenoemde factoren kan worden verklaard. Alhoewel de factoren dus een goede verklaring bieden, lijkt hun verklarende kracht wel afhankelijk van de sociale, historische en culturele context van een land. Factoren die binnen landen nog gerelateerd zijn aan de acceptatie, zijn bijvoorbeeld de lokale en nationale homo-beweging, moreel leiderschap van invloedrijke personen en de zichtbaarheid van homoseksualiteit in een samenleving en de nationale media.

Kanttekeningen

Het huidige rapport laat zien dat Europa op weg is naar een grotere sociale acceptatie van homoseksualiteit, maar dat er grote verschillen zijn tussen landen naar startpositie, de grootte van de verandering en het doorzetten van de trend. Ook is ingegaan op het feit dat veranderingen in de houding ten opzichte van homoseksualiteit niet in een sociaal of historisch vacuüm plaatsvinden, maar samengaan met bredere moderniseringsprocessen (bijv. stijgende opleidingsniveaus), religieuze factoren en politieke ontwikkelingen. Het rapport kent een aantal beperkingen. De gebruikte datasets zijn de meest betrouwbare die op dit moment voorhanden zijn, maar er kleven toch een aantal nadelen aan. Zo worden er slechts één of twee vragen over homoseksualiteit gesteld, waardoor niet goed in kaart gebracht kan worden of de houdingen verschillen voor verschillende onderwerpen (bijv. de houding ten opzichte van het openstellen van het huwelijk of adoptie door paren van gelijk geslacht). Ook bevatten de onderzoeken geen vragen over de acceptatie van specifieke groepen. De vragen zijn algemeen gesteld en hebben betrekking op homoseksuele mannen en, soms, op lesbische vrouwen maar of er verschillen zijn in de acceptatie van die groepen is niet bekend. Transgenders en biseksuelen komen bovendien in deze enquêtes helemaal niet aan bod.

Aanbevelingen

De houding van de bevolking kan van invloed zijn op politieke besluiten over de rechten van LHBS. Verschillende sociale klimaten vragen om een verschillende aanpak vragen bij het bevorderen van gelijke rechten voor deze groep. Andere aanbevelingen gelden voor toekomstig onderzoek. Dit zou meer rekening moeten houden met de diversiteit binnen de doelgroep (bijv. verschillen in houding ten opzichte van lesbische vrouwen en homoseksuele mannen, houdingen ten aanzien van transgenders) en moeten onderzoeken welke rol de afkeer van gender non-conformiteit speelt bij een negatieve attitude ten opzichte van homoseksualiteit.

Tolerantie in de toekomst

Of Europa zich naar meer tolerantie gaat bewegen in de toekomst, is nog maar de vraag. Aan de ene kant zijn er redenen om aan te nemen dat de acceptatie van homoseksualiteit verder zal toenemen. Immers, het gemiddelde opleidingsniveau stijgt, steeds minder mensen wonen in kleine plattelandsgemeenten, de duur van EU lidmaatschappen neemt toe en de mogelijkheden om (online) aan te sluiten bij de wereldwijde 'civil society' en homobeweging nemen in rap tempo toe. Ook zijn er verscheidene Europese landen, instituties en regels die voor meer gelijkwaardigheid voor LHB burgers in Europa opkomen. Deze factoren kunnen bijdragen aan een verder toenemende acceptatie van homoseksualiteit.
Er zijn echter tegelijkertijd minstens twee belangrijke redenen om aan te nemen dat niet zeker is dat de sociale acceptatie overal toe zal nemen. Ten eerste houdt de economische crisis flink huis in Europa. De werkeloosheidcijfers stijgen, inkomens dalen en – afhankelijk van het gevoerde beleid – inkomensverschillen worden groter. Dit zijn factoren die samengaan met minder sociale acceptatie. Als een land in politieke of economische zwaardere tijden verkeerd, zijn mensen geneigd om zich te richten op traditionele waarden die zekerheid bieden en zich te bekommeren om fysieke en economische behoeften. Dit gaat vaak ten koste van een tolerante houding ten opzichte van minderheden, waaronder homoseksuele mannen, lesbische vrouwen, biseksuelen en transgenders.

De tweede reden om vraagtekens te plaatsen bij een toenemende acceptatie van homo-seksualiteit is het verschijnsel dat bij een toenemende globalisering, mensen vaak lokale en nationale gebruiken willen beschermen. Tradities en waarden die men bij het eigen land vindt horen wil men behouden, terwijl zaken die worden ervaren als 'iets dat moet van Europa' worden verworpen. Als dit proces zich ook voor doet op gebied van accepta-tie van homoseksualiteit, dan kan het zijn dat landen met een negatieve houding in ver-leden en heden blijven vasthouden aan deze intolerantie. Door anti-EU sentimenten kan daar de houding binnen bepaalde groepen wellicht zelfs negatiever worden.

Appendix A Country abbreviations

Country code	Country	Country code	Country
AL	Albania	IE	Ireland
AM	Armenia	IS	Iceland
AT	Austria	IT	Italy
AZ	Azerbaijan	LT	Latvia
BA	Bosnia-Herzegovina	LU	Luxembourg
BE	Belgium	LV	Lithuania
BG	Bulgaria	MD	Moldova
BY	Belarus	ME	Montenegro
CH	Switzerland	MK	Macedonia
CY	Cyprus	MT	Malta
CY-TCC	Northern Cyprus	NL	Netherlands
CZ	Czech Republic	NO	Norway
DE	Germany	PL	Poland
DK	Denmark	PT	Portugal
EE	Estonia	RO	Romania
ES	Spain	RS	Serbia
FI	Finland	RS-KM	Kosovo
FR	France	RU	Russian Federation
GB-GBN	Great Britain	SE	Sweden
GB-NIR	Northern Ireland	SI	Slovenia
GE	Georgia	SK	Slovak Republic
GR	Greece	TR	Turkey
HR	Croatia	UA	Ukraine
HU	Hungary		

Appendix B Additional tables chapter 2

Indications of significance of changes in attitude towards justification of homosexuality. A + indicates
a significant increase in tolerant attitudes between the two years; a – indicates a significant decrease
in tolerant attitudes between the two years; and a ∞ indicates no change in attitudes between the two
years. A blank space indicates that in that year, the country did not take part in the data collection.
Norway did not collect data in 1999, so the change between 1990 and 2008 was examined

	1981 to 1990	1990 to 1999	1999 to 2008
Northern Europe	+	+	+
Iceland	+	+	+
Norway	+		+
Sweden	∞	+	∞
Finland		+	+
Denmark	–	+	+
Western Europe	+	+	+
The Netherlands	+	+	∞
Belgium	+	+	+
Germany	+	+	∞
France	+	+	+
Great Britain	∞	+	+
Ireland	+	+	+
Northern Ireland	+	+	∞
Austria		+	∞
Central/Eastern Europe		+	∞
Poland		+	∞
Bulgaria		+	∞
Romania		+	+
Czech Republic		+	–
Slovak Republic		+	∞
Slovenia		+	–
Hungary		–	+
Estonia		+	–
Latvia		∞	+
Lithuania		+	∞
Southern Europe	+	+	+
Italy	+	+	
Spain	+	+	+
Portugal		+	+
Malta		+	+

Source: EVS '81; EVS '90; EVS '99; EVS '08

Table B.2

Indications of significance of changes in attitude on whether the respondent would not want to have homosexual neighbours. A + indicates a significant increase in tolerant attitudes between the two years; a – indicates a significant decrease in tolerant attitudes between the two years; and a ∞ indicates no change in attitudes between the two years. A blank space indicates that in that year, the country did not take part in the data collection.

	1990 to 1999	1999 to 2008
Northern Europe	+	+
Iceland	+	+
Sweden	+	∞
Finland	∞	+
Denmark	+	∞
Western Europe	+	+
The Netherlands	+	–
Belgium	+	+
Germany	+	–
France	+	+
Great Britain	+	+
Ireland	+	+
Northern Ireland	+	∞
Austria	+	∞
Central/Eastern Europe	+	+
Poland	+	∞
Bulgaria	+	∞
Romania	+	+
Czech Republic	+	∞
Slovak Republic	+	+
Slovenia	∞	+
Estonia	+	∞
Latvia	+	∞
Lithuania	+	∞
Southern Europe	+	+
Italy	+	∞
Spain	+	+
Portugal	+	∞
Malta	∞	+

Source: EVS'90; EVS'99; EVS'08

Table B.3

Indications of significance of changes in attitude on whether gay men and lesbians should be free to live their lives as they wish. A + indicates a significant increase in tolerant attitudes between the two years; a – indicates a significant decrease in tolerant attitudes between the two years; and a ∞ indicates no change in attitudes between the two years. A blank space indicates that in that year, the country did not take part in the data collection. The Czech Republic and Greece did not collect data in 2006, so the changes between 2004 and 2008 were examined.

	2002 to 2004	2004 to 2006	2006 to 2008	2008 to 2010
Northern Europe	+	∞	+	+
Norway	+	∞	∞	+
Sweden	+	+	∞	+
Finland	+	∞	+	∞
Denmark	∞	∞	+	∞
Western Europe	∞	∞	+	+
Netherlands	∞	∞	+	+
Belgium	∞	∞	+	∞
Germany	∞	∞	+	∞
France	∞	∞	+	–
Great Britain	+	∞	∞	+
Ireland	–	∞	+	
Austria	∞	∞		
Switzerland	–	∞	+	∞
Central/Eastern Europe	–	–	+	+
Poland	∞	+	∞	∞
Russian Federation			∞	∞
Ukraine		–	∞	
Bulgaria			–	+
Czech Republic	∞		+	∞
Slovak Republic		∞	∞	
Slovenia	∞	∞	∞	∞
Hungary	∞	∞	∞	∞
Estonia		–	+	∞
Southern Europe	∞	+	∞	+
Greece	∞		∞	
Spain	–	+	+	∞
Portugal	–	∞	∞	–

Source: ESS '02, '04, '06, '08, '10

Appendix C Multi-level analysis

Table C.1

factor	model 1	model 2	model 3	model 4	model 5	model 6	model 7
female		0.850***	0.822***	0.946***	0.901***	0.874***	0.524***
self-expression values (ref. materialist)							
mixed		0.618***	0.533***	0.486***	0.438***	0.429***	0.294***
post-materialist		1.587***	1.339***	1.239***	1.202***	1.152***	0.767***
unemployed		0.523***	0.527***	0.470***	0.182**	0.176**	0.199***
income		0.244***	0.147***	0.131***	0.074***	0.083***	0.047***
GDP per capita		0.000***	0.000***	0.000***	0.000***	0.000	0.000
GINI		-0.087*	-0.088*	-0.105*	-0.108*	-0.141***	-0.123***
urbanization			0.112***	0.104***	0.103***	0.101***	0.082***
education (ref. low)							
middle			0.877***	0.735***	0.462***	0.469***	0.236***
high			1.414***	1.289***	1.049***	1.054***	0.566***
religious denomination (ref. no denomination)							
free				-1.059***	-1.122***	-1.036***	-0.946***
muslim				-1.746***	-2.215***	-2.289***	-1.698***
orthodox				-0.433***	-0.425***	-0.453***	-0.209
various				-1.024***	-1.010***	-1.022***	-0.764***
protestant				-0.163*	-0.091	-0.045	-0.009
roman catholic				-0.361***	-0.292***	-0.246***	-0.064
importance religion				0.452***	0.359***	0.337***	0.179***
religion country (ref. no majority)							
> 70% roman catholic				-0.421	-0.578	-0.510	-0.181
> 70% protestant				-0.524	-0.510	-0.165	-0.783*
> 70% orthodox				0.367	0.133	0.356	0.410
> 70% no religion				-1.364*	-1.379*	-0.748	-0.150
age (ref. 15-24)							
25-34					-0.094	-0.089	-0.073
35-44					-0.441***	-0.445***	-0.444***
45-54					-0.646***	-0.657***	-0.585***
54-65					-0.975***	-0.989***	-0.833***
> 65					-1.575***	-1.572***	-1.199***

Table C.1   (continued)

factor	model 1	model 2	model 3	model 4	model 5	model 6	model 7
political orientation						-0.114***	-0.079***
communist past						-1.295**	-1.314***
length of EU membership						0.011	0.008
attitude towards gender							-9.702***
Gender Equality Index							0.034
% unexplained variance							
at country level	28.8	7.2	7.7	7.0	7.9	5.3	2.8

a   Higher scores indicate higher income.
b   Higher GDP indicates more country-level income.
c   Higher GINI indicates more income inequality within a country.
d   Higher scores indicate more urbanized residential areas.
e   Higher scores indicate more importance attached to religion.
f   Higher scores indicate more political affiliation with right wing.
g   Higher scores indicate more conservative gender attitudes.
h   Higher GEI indicates more gender equality in education, economic participation and power.
The dependent variable is the attitude towards justification of homosexuality; higher scores indicate more justification.

Notes

1   Although we are aware that the LGBT community (lesbian, gay, bisexual and transgender individuals) also includes people with different gender identities and gender expressions, we will be talking about LGB individuals in this report since no long-term European data are available for transgender individuals. Talking about LGBT individuals would merely mask this shortcoming.

2   We refer in this report to attitudes towards homosexuality, since this is the way most items in the EVS and ESS were framed and no questions on bisexuality are included in the EVS or ESS.

3   The findings will be presented on the basis of currently existing countries. This means that figures for the Slovak Republic and Czech Republic will be presented separately, even though during the first rounds of EVS data collection these countries still formed one country (Czechoslovakia). One figure will be presented for Germany, even though Germany was two countries during the first round of EVS data collection.

4   Data were also collected in Azerbaijan and Kosovo, but ESS guidelines were not followed in these countries and they are therefore excluded from the analyses discussed here.

5   Of course, it is debatable in which region some countries should be placed (e.g. Estonia could be North or Central/East, Slovenia could be in the South or Central/East, Austria could be in West or Central/East, etc.).

6   In 2008, Italy used a different formulation for the question on justification of homosexuality. Italian figures are therefore missing for 2008. Norway did not take part in the 1999 wave of the EVS.

7   When interpreting the percentages, it should be borne in mind that there are differences between countries in the occurrence of missing values. For example, on average around 5% of respondents in the 2008 EVS round did not answer the question or answered 'don't know'. In some countries this percentage is much higher (e.g. above 10% in Sweden, the Slovak Republic, Portugal, Malta and Bulgaria) while in others it is much lower (e.g. around 2% in Norway, France, Belgium and Denmark). This might influence the reported percentages. In the present study, missing answers and respondents indicating that they do not know are coded as missing values.

8   Hungary used a different formulation for the question on homosexual neighbours and Hungarian figures are therefore missing. Norway did not take part in the 1999 wave of the EVS. Since this leaves data for only two EVS waves for Hungary and Norway, these countries were excluded from these analyses altogether.

9   When interpreting the percentages, it should be borne in mind that there are differences between countries in the occurrence of missing values. This might influence the reported percentages. See also note 7.

10 When interpreting the percentages, it should be borne in mind that there are differences between countries in the occurrence of missing values. This might influence the reported percentages. A study of the missing value data in ESS 2002, 2004, and 2006 indicated that differences in missing values are mainly caused by participants answering 'don't know' and that the percentage of missing values is related to the method of survey completion (computer-assisted or pencil and paper) (Koch and Blohm 2009)

11   It remains to be seen whether this holds true for Austria, which reported 72% tolerance in 2006 and did not subsequently participate in the ESS.

12 Not all countries completed all three questions. For example, Malta and Iceland were not included in the ESS, while Russia and Ukraine were not included in the EVS.

13 Correlations of .50 (or -.50) or higher are seen as indicative of a strong relationship; correlations between .30 and .50 (or -30 and -.50) are perceived as a medium relationship; and correlations between .10 and .30 (-.30 and -.10) are regarded as a weak or very weak relationship.

14 The factors were constructed by means of a confirmatory factor analyses.

15 The selection was based on the relevance of the content and availability for 2008.

16 GEI scores were not available for all countries in 2008.

17 Hofstede scores were not available for all countries.

18 For the analyses, the Hofstede scores presented on the website www.geert-hofstede.com were used. Taras et al. (2012) calculated new standardized scores based on meta-analyses. When using their scores, correlations are somewhat higher but remain in the low range, and the same diverse pattern was found (i.e. feminine countries with tolerant attitudes, masculine countries with intolerant attitudes, but also vice versa). The number of countries that could be included in these analyses was more limited, and we have therefore opted to use the scores from the website.

19 When interpreting the strength and magnitude of the relationships, it is important to take into account that relationships between country-level issues such as public attitudes are relatively high because they ignore variation within countries.

20 The reason for this is that there are no data available from 1981 till 2008 for all included measures (e.g. Social Watch started with the Gender Equality Index in 2007; not all gender attitudes were included in the earlier waves of EVS).

21 It is important to note that these results should not be interpreted as providing proof that some findings of previous studies (e.g. concerning GDP or religion) are not correct. The deviating results are likely to be related to differences in measurements and differences in the included countries and factors. Inclusion or exclusion of certain factors exerts an influence on the relevance of other factors. Since previous studies have included different factors, different measures and different countries, it is not surprising that they yield different results. If anything, the analysis here shows the importance of a well-designed model for including or excluding certain factors and countries.

22 Indicators of education, urbanization, religion, etc. are taken from the EVS data set and might not be comparable with official macrolevel indicators from the OECD or Eurostat, for example.

23 Linda Freimane and Juris Lavrikovs (ILGA-Europe).

References

Adam, B.D., J.W. Duyvendak and A. Krouwel (1999). Gay and Lesbian Movements beyond Borders. National Imprints of a Worldwide Movement. In: B.D. Adam, J.W. Duyvendak and A. Krouwel (eds.), *The Global Emergence of Gay and Lesbian Politics. National Imprints of a Worldwide Movement* (p. 344-371). Philadelphia: Temple University Press.

Adamczyk, A. and C. Pitt (2009). Shaping attitudes about homosexuality: The role of religion and cultural context. In: *Social Science Research*, vol. 38, no. 2, p. 338-351.

Anderson, R. and T. Fetner (2008a). Cohort differences in tolerance of homosexuality. Attitudinal change in Canada and the United States, 1981-2000. In: *Public Opinion Quarterly*, vol. 72, no. 2, p. 311-330.

Anderson, R. and T. Fetner (2008b). Economic inequality and intolerance: Attitudes towards homosexuality in 35 democracies. In: *American Journal of Political Science*, vol. 52, no. 4, p. 942-958.

Akker, H. van den, R. van der Ploeg and P. Scheepers (2012). Disapproval of homosexuality: Comparative research on individual and national determinants of disapproval of homosexuality in 20 European countries. In: *International Journal of Public Opinion Research*. Online publication ahead of print.

Bernat, J.A., K.S. Calhoun, H.E. Adams and A. Zeichner (2001). Homophobia and physical aggression toward homosexual and heterosexual individuals. In: *Journal of Abnormal Psychology*, vol. 110, no. 1, p. 179-187.

Bos, D. (2010). *De aard, de daad en het woord. Een halve eeuw opinie- en besluitvorming over homoseksualiteit in Protestants Nederland.* Den Haag: Sociaal en Cultureel Planbureau.

Brewer, P.R. (2003). The sifting foundations of public opinion about gay rights. In: *The Journal of Politics*, vol. 65, no. 4, p. 1208-1220.

Bröer, C. (2006). *Beleid vormt overlast. Hoe beleidsdiscoursen de beleving van geluid bepalen.* Amsterdam: Aksant.

Carneiro, N.S. and I. Menezes (2007). From an Oppressed Citizenship to Affirmative Identities: Lesbian and Gay Political Participation in Portugal. In: *Journal of Homosexuality*, vol. 35, no. 3, p. 65-82.

Castles, F.G. and H. Obinger (2008). Worlds, families, regimes: Country clusters in European and OECD area public policy. In: *West European Politics*, vol. 31, no. 1/2, p. 321-344.

Chetaille, A. (2011). Poland: Sovereignty and Sexuality in Post-Socialist Times. In: M. Tremblay, D. Paternotte and C. Johnson (eds.), *The Lesbian and Gay Movement and the State. Comparative Insights into a Transformed Relationship* (p. 119-133). Farnham: Ashgate Publishing Limited.

Czarnecki, G.E. (2007) Analogies of Pre-War Anti-Semitism and Present-day Homophobia in Poland. In: R. Kuhar and J. Takács (eds.), *Beyond the Pink Curtain. Everyday Life of LGBT people in Eastern Europe* (p. 327-344). Ljubljana: The Peace Institute.

European Commission (2008). *Discrimination in the European Union: Perception, experiences and attitudes.* Accessed online February 5, 2013 at http://ec.europa.eu/public_opinion/archives/ebs/ebs_296_en.pdf

European Commission (2009). *Special Eurobarometer 317. Discrimination in the EU in 2009.* Accessed online February 5, 2013 at http://ec.europa.eu/public_opinion/archives/ebs/ebs_317_en.pdf

European Commission (2012). *Special Eurobarometer 393. Discrimination in the EU in 2012.* Accessed online February 5, 2013 at http://ec.europa.eu/public_opinion/archives/ebs/ebs_393_en.pdf

FRA (2008). *Homophobia and Discrimination on Grounds of Sexual Orientation in the EU Member States Part I – Legal Analysis.* Vienna: European Union Agency for Fundamental Rights.

FRA (2009). *Homophobia and discrimination on grounds of sexual orientation and gender identity in the EU member states: Part II – The social situation.* Vienna: European Union Agency for Fundamental Rights.

FRA (2011). *Homophobia, transphobia and discrimination on grounds of sexual orientation and gender identity in the EU Member States.* Vienna: European Union Agency for Fundamental Rights.

Franklin, K. (2000). Antigay Behaviors Among Young Adults. Prevalence, Patterns, and Motivators in a Noncriminal Population. In: *Journal of Interpersonal Violence,* vol. 15, no. 4, p. 339-362.

Gerhards, J. (2010). Non-discrimination towards homosexuality. The European Union's policy and citizens' attitudes towards homosexuality in 27 European countries. In: *International Sociology,* vol. 25, no. 1, p. 5-28.

Graaf, P.M. de (2008). *Waarden die er toe doen. De European Value Study in de 21e eeuw* (oratie). Tilburg: Tilburg University.

Gruszczynska, A. (2007). Living 'La Vida' Internet: Some Notes on the Cyberization of Polish LGBT Community. In: R. Kuhar and J. Takacs (eds.), *Beyond the Pink Curtain. Everyday Life of LGBT people in Eastern Europe* (p. 95-115). Ljubljana: The Peace Institute.

Hadler, M. (2012). The influence of world societal forces on social tolerance. A time comparative study of prejudices in 32 countries. In: *The Sociological Quarterly,* vol. 53, no. 1, p. 211-237.

Helfer, L.R. and E. Voeten (2013). International courts as agents of legal change: Evidence from LGBT rights in Europe. In: *International Organization,* vol. 67, 2013. Accessed online February 5, 2013 at http://ssrn.com/abstract=1850526

Hooghe, M. and C. Meeusen (2012). Homophobia and the transition to adulthood: A three year panel study among Belgian late adolescents and young adults, 2008-2011. In: *Journal of Youth and Adolescence,* vol. 41, no. 9, p. 1197-1207.

Huijnk, W. and J. Dagevos (2012). *Dichter bij elkaar?* The Hague: The Netherlands Institute for Social Research.

Inglehart, R. (1977). *The silent revolution. Changing values and political styles among western publics.* Princeton: Princeton University Press.

Koch, A. and M. Blohm (2009). Item nonresponse in the European Social Survey. In: *Research & Methods,* vol. 18, no. 1., p. 45-65.

Kowalska, A. (2011). Polish Queer Lesbianism: Sexual Identity Without a Lesbian Community. In: *Journal of Lesbian Studies,* vol. 15 no. 3, p. 324-336.

Keinz, A. (2011). European Desires and National Bedrooms? Negotiating "Normalcy" in Postsocialist Poland. In: *Central European History,* vol. 44, no. 1, p. 92-117.

Keuzenkamp, S. (2011). *Acceptance of homosexuality in The Netherlands. International comparison, trends and current situation.* The Hague: The Netherlands Institute for Social Research.

Keuzenkamp, S. and D. Bos (2007). *Out in the Netherlands. Acceptance of homosexuality in the Netherlands.* The Hague: The Netherlands Institute for Social Research.

Keuzenkamp, S. and L. Kuyper (2013). *Acceptance of homosexual, lesbian, bisexual, and transgender individuals in the Netherlands 2013.* The Hague: The Netherlands Institute for Social Research.

Kuyper, L. (2012). Transgenders in Nederland: Prevalentie en attitude. In: *Tijdschrift voor Seksuologie,* vol. 36, no. 2, p. 129-135.

Lax, J.R. and J.H. Philips (2009). Gay rights in the United States: Public opinion and policy responsiveness. In: *American Political Science Review,* vol. 103, no. 3, p. 367-386.

Lisdonk, J. van and N. Kooiman (2012). Biseksualiteit: Vele gezichten en tegelijkertijd onzichtbaar. In: S. Keuzenkamp, N. Kooiman and J. van Lisdonk, *Niet te ver uit de kast* (p. 78-99). The Hague: The Netherlands Institute for Social Research.

Llamas, R. and F. Vila (1999). Passion for Life: A History of the Lesbian and Gay Movement in Spain. In: B.D. Adam, J.W. Duyvendak and A. Krouwel (eds.), *The Global Emergence of Gay and Lesbian Politics. National Imprints of a Worldwide Movement* (p. 214-241). Philadelphia: Temple University Press.

Loftus, J. (2001). America's liberalization in attitudes towards homosexuality, 1973-1998. In: *American Sociological Review*, vol. 66, No. 5, p. 762-782.

Long, S. (1999). Gay and Lesbian Movements in Eastern Europe: Romania, Hungary, and the Czech Republic. In: B.D. Adam, J.W. Duyvendak and A. Krouwel (eds.), *The Global Emergence of Gay and Lesbian Politics. National Imprints of a Worldwide Movement* (p. 242-265). Philadelphia: Temple University Press.

López Penedo, S. (2012). Queer Politics in Spain: There is Life after Same-Sex Marriage Legislation. In: *Jindal Global Law Review*, vol. 4, no. 1, p. 238-263.

Meerendonk, B. van de and P. Scheepers (2006). Denial of equal civil rights for lesbians and gay men in the Netherlands, 1980-1993. In: *Journal of Homosexuality*, vol. 47, no. 2, p. 63-80.

Meeusen, C. and M. Hooghe (2012). *Does same-sex marriage legislation have an impact on tolerance of homosexuality? Trends in attitudes toward homosexuality in European countries between 2002-2010* (paper presented at the International Conference on the European Social Survey, November 23-25 2012). Nicosia: Republic of Cyprus.

McVeigh, R. and M.D. Diaz (2009). Voting to ban same-sex marriage: Interests, values, and communities. In: *American Sociological Review*, vol. 74, no. 6, p. 891-915.

Moeller, R.G. (2010). Private Acts, Public Anxieties, and the Fight to Decriminalize Male Homosexuality in West Germany. In: *Feminist Studies*, vol. 36, no. 3, p. 528-552.

Nierman, A.J., S.C. Thompson, A. Bryan and A.L. Mahaffey (2007). Gender Role Beliefs and Attitudes toward Lesbians and Gay Men in Chile and the U.S. In: *Sex Roles*, vol. 57, no. 1/2, p. 61-67.

Ohrlander, J., J. Batalova and J. Treas (2005). Explaining educational influences on attitudes toward homosexual relations. In: *Social Science Research*, vol. 34, no. 4, p. 781-799.

Patel, S., T.E. Long, S.L. McCammon and K.L. Wuensch (1995). Personality and emotional correlates of self-reported antigay behaviors. In: *Journal of Interpersonal Violence*, vol. 10, no. 3, p. 354-366.

Parrott, D.J. (2008). A theoretical framework for antigay aggression: Review of established hypothesized effects within the context of the general aggression model. In: *Clinical Psychology Review*, vol. 28, no. 6, p. 933-951.

Pierson, P. (1993). When effect becomes cause: Policy feedback and political change. In: *World Politics*, vol. 45, no. 4, p. 595-628.

Pollock, P.H. (1994). Issues, values, and critical moments: Did "Magic" Johnson transform public opinion on AIDS? In: *American Journal of Political Science*, vol. 38, no. 2, p. 426-446.

Riggle, E.D.B., S.S. Rostosky and S. Horne (2010). Does it matter where you live? Nondiscrimination laws and the experiences of LGB residents. In: *Sexuality Research and Social Policy*, vol. 7, no. 3, p. 168-175.

Schuyf, J. and A. Krouwel (1999). The Dutch Lesbian and Gay Movement: The Politics of Accommodation. In: B.D. Adam, J.W. Duyvendak and A. Krouwel (eds.), *The Global Emergence of Gay and Lesbian Politics. National Imprints of a Worldwide Movement* (p. 158-184). Philadelphia: Temple University Press.

Sherkat, D.E., M. Powell-Williams, G. Maddox and K.M. de Vries (2011). Religion, politics, and support for same-sex marriage in the United States, 1988-2008. In: *Social Science Research*, vol. 40, no. 1, p. 167-180.

Štulhofer, A. and I. Rimic (2009). Determinants of homonegativity in Europe. In: *Journal of Sex Research*, vol. 46, no. 1, p. 24-32.

Szulc, L. (2011). Queer in Poland: Under Construction. In: L. Downing and R. Gillett (eds.), *Queer in Europe. Contemporary Case Studies* (p. 159-172). Franhem/Burlington: Ashgate Publishing Company.

Takács, J. and I. Szalma (2011). Homophobia and same-sex partnership legislation in Europe. In: *Equality Diversity and Inclusion: An International Journal*, vol. 30, no. 5, p. 356-378.

Taras, V., P. Steel and B.L. Kirkman (2012). Improving national cultural indices using a longitudinal meta-analysis of Hofstede's dimensions. In: *Journal of World Business*, vol. 47, no. 3, p. 329-341.

TK (2010/2011). *Hoofdlijnen Emancipatiebeleid 2011-2015*. Tweede Kamer, vergaderjaar 2010/2011, 27017, nr. 74.

Yang, A.S. (1997). Trends: Attitudes Toward Homosexuality. In: *The Public Opinion Quarterly*, vol. 61, no. 3, p. 477-507.

Publications of the Netherlands Institute for Social Research | scp in English

Sport in the Netherlands (2007). Annet Tiessen-Raaphorst, Koen Breedveld. ISBN 978 90 377 0302 3

Market Place Europe. Fifty years of public opinion and market integration in the European Union. European Outlook 5 (2007). Paul Dekker, Albert van der Horst, Henk Kox, Arjan Lejour, Bas Straathof, Peter Tammes, Charlotte Wennekers. ISBN 978 90 377 0306 1

Explaining Social Exclusion. A theoretical model tested in the Netherlands (2007). Gerda Jehoel-Gijsbers, Cok Vrooman. ISBN 978 90 377 0325 2

Out in the Netherlands. Acceptance of homosexuality in the Netherlands (2007). Saskia Keuzenkamp, David Bos. ISBN 978 90 377 0324 5

Comparing Care. The care of the elderly in ten EU-countries (2007). Evert Pommer, Isolde Woittiez, John Stevens. ISBN 978 90 377 0303 0

Beyond the breadline (2008). Arjan Soede, Cok Vrooman. ISBN 978 90 377 0371 9

Facts and Figures of the Netherlands. Social and Cultural Trends 1995-2006 (2008). Theo Roes (ed.). ISBN 978 90 377 0211 8

Self-selection bias versus nonresponse bias in the Perceptions of Mobility survey. A comparison using multiple imputation (2008). Daniel Oberski. ISBN 978 90 377 0343 6

The future of the Dutch public library: ten years on (2008). Frank Huysmans, Carlien Hillebrink. ISBN 978 90 377 0380 1

Europe's Neighbours. European neighbourhood policy and public opinion on the European Union. European Outlook 6 (2008). Paul Dekker, Albert van der Horst, Suzanne Kok, Lonneke van Noije, Charlotte Wennekers. ISBN 978 90 377 0386 3

Values on a grey scale. Elderly Policy Monitor 2008 (2008). Cretien van Campen (ed.). ISBN 978 90 377 0392 4

The Netherlands Institute for Social Research | scp at a glance. Summaries of 16 scp-research projects in 2008 (2009). ISBN 978 90 377 0413 6

Sport in the Netherlands (2009). Annet Tiessen-Raaphorst, Koen Breedveld. ISBN 978 90 377 0428 0

Strategic Europe. Markets and power in 2030 and public opinion on the European Union (2009). Paul Dekker, Albert van der Horst, Paul Koutstaal, Henk Kox, Tom van der Meer, Charlotte Wennekers, Teunis Brosens, Bas Verschoor. ISBN 978 90 377 0440 2

Building Inclusion. Housing and Integration of Ethnic Minorities in the Netherlands (2009).
Jeanet Kullberg, Isik Kulu-Glasgow. ISBN 978 90 377 0442 6

Making up the Gap, Migrant Education in the Netherlands (2009). Lex Herweijer.
ISBN 978 90 377 0433 4

Rules of Relief. Institutions of social security, and their impact (2009). J.C. Vrooman.
ISBN 978 90 377 0218 7

Integration in ten trends (2010). Jaco Dagevos and Mérove Gijsberts. ISBN 78 90 377 0472 3

Monitoring acceptance of homosexuality in the Netherlands (2010). Saskia Keuzenkamp.
ISBN 978 90 377 484 6

The minimum agreed upon. Consensual budget standards for the Netherlands (2010). Stella Hoff, Arjan
Soede, Cok Vrooman, Corinne van Gaalen, Albert Luten, Sanne Lamers.
ISBN 978 90 377 0472 3

The Social State of the Netherlands 2009 (2010). Rob Bijl, Jeroen Boelhouwer, Evert Pommer,
Peggy Schyns (eds.). ISBN 978 90 377 0466 2

*At home in the Netherlands. Trends in integration of non-Western migrants. Annual report on Integration
2009* (2010). Mérove Gijsberts and Jaco Dagevos. ISBN 978 90 377 0487 7

In the spotlight: informal care in the Netherlands (2010). Debbie Oudijk, Alice de Boer, Isolde Woittiez, Joost Timmermans, Mirjam de Klerk. ISBN 978 90 377 0497 6

Wellbeing in the Netherlands. The SCP life situation index since 1974 (2010). Jeroen Boelhouwer.
ISBN 978 90 377 0345 0

Just different, that's all. Acceptance of homosexuality in the Netherlands (2010). Saskia Keuzenkamp et
al. (ed.) ISBN 978 90 377 0502 7

*Acceptance of homosexuality in the Netherlands 2011. International comparison, trends and current situa-
tion* (2011). Saskia Keuzenkamp. ISBN 978 90 377 0580 5

*Living together apart. Ethnic concentration in the neighbourhood and ethnic minorities' social contacts and
language practices* (2011). Miranda Vervoort. ISBN 978 377 0552 2

Frail older persons in the Netherlands. Summary (2011). Cretien van Campen (ed.) ISBN 978 90 377
0563 8

Frail older persons in the Netherlands (2011). Cretien van Campen (ed.) ISBN 978 90 377 0553 9

Measuring and monitoring immigrant integration in Europe (2012). Rob Bijl and Arjen Verweij (eds.)
ISBN 978 90 377 0569 0

The Social State of the Netherlands 2011. Summary (2012). Rob Bijl, Jeroen Boelhouwer, Mariëlle Cloïn, Evert Pommer (eds.) ISBN 978 90 377 0605 5

Countries compared on public performance. A study of public sector performance in 28 countries (2012). Jedid-Jah Jonker (ed.) ISBN 978 90 377 0584 3

A day with the Dutch. Time use in the Netherlands and fifteen other European countries (2012). Mariëlle Cloïn. ISBN 978 90 377 0606 2

Acceptance of lesbian, gay, bisexual and transgender individuals in the Netherlands 2013 (2013). Saskia Keuzenkamp and Lisette Kuyper. ISBN 978 90 377 0649 9

Towards Tolerance. Exploring changes and explaining differences in attitudes towards homosexuality in Europe (2013). Lisette Kuyper, Jurjen Iedema, Saskia Keuzenkamp. ISBN 978 90 377 0650 5